Mended will show you how to create an incredible, God-honoring legacy for your family. This is an amazing resource for anyone who desires to deepen their mother-daughter relationship in a biblical, healthy, and healed way.

Lysa TerKeurst, *New York Times* bestselling author and
president of Proverbs 31 Ministries

If you're ready to deepen and strengthen your relationship with your mother, your daughter, your mother-in-law, or your daughter-in-law, *Mended* offers the practical, biblical guidance and wise, heartfelt encouragement you're looking for. Whether you struggle with past hurts or present disappointments, Helen and Blythe make it clear that "no one and no relationship is beyond hope." Each suggestion is supported with Scripture and wrapped in real-life examples drawn from two different generations. So helpful, so hope-filled, so healing!

Liz Curtis Higgs, bestselling author of *Bad Girls of the Bible*

Helen and Blythe have bared their souls and brightened our relational paths with their writing of this soul-searching, life-instructing book. They walked through fire as they wrote, and the results have emerged as pure gold.

Jan Silvious, author of *Courage for the Unknown Season*
and *Fool-Proofing Your Life*

Blythe and Helen weave godly, practical suggestions to move the relationship with your mother or daughter from harmful to healed. In a beautiful conversation, the duo teaches the reader how to sow seeds of peace rather than discord by pointing her to the Author of reconciliation, Jesus.

Wendy Pope, Proverbs 31 Ministries speaker
and author of *Wait and See*

The mother-daughter relationship can be both a place where we are most comfortable and vulnerable and yet, at times, feel as though we are walking a tight rope. This practical guide gives us the tools to navigate nurturing and restoring this most important relationship. It will be a resource that I will refer to over and over again.

Lynn Cowell, Proverbs 31 Ministries speaker and author of *Make Your Move*

I cannot think of two women who embody transparency, courage, strength, and wisdom more than Blythe Daniel and Helen McIntosh. As you read this book, you'll surely be soaked in their special kind of wonderful, and your own mother-daughter relationships will be saturated in the love of Jesus—the mender of our souls.

LaTan Roland Murphy, author of *Courageous Women of the Bible*

I vacillated back and forth between mother and daughter as I read *Mended*—learning as a mother, absorbing as a daughter. These words can unlock those of us who have felt stuck within either role, unsure of how to find a new way out of old patterns. God's heart for healing families lies within these pages.

Sara Hagerty, author of *Every Bitter Thing Is Sweet* and *Unseen*

Whether your desire is to mend a strained and broken relationship or simply to make a strong and healthy one even better, you will find yourself enlightened, encouraged, and expectant about the future through the pages of *Mended*. I highly encourage mothers and daughters to enjoy this beautiful book together.

Jeannie Cunnion, author of *Mom Set Free*

As the mother of five daughters, I know firsthand how important the mother-daughter relationship is and how much cultivating is necessary to keep good lines of communication open—the prerequisite for a healthy relationship. In my experience hurts and wounds are inevitable between mothers and daughters. But alienation is not. In *Mended*, we are given a proven path to repair the brokenness and build upon the beauty that is present.

Gail Hyatt, wife of Michael Hyatt, *New York Times* bestselling author of *Platform*

Blythe McIntosh Daniel and Helen McIntosh gently move us through the mending process by sharing practical tips steeped in grace and compassion. This book will equip you with the tools you need to heal the relationship with your mother or daughter as you look to Jesus for wisdom and discernment. Blythe and Helen paint a beautiful picture of hope and help for mending your relationships.

Connie Albers, author of *Parenting Beyond the Rules*

If you have ever thought, "I wish I knew how to really talk to my mom, to my daughter," this book will be a gift. So often we allow years to pass, stuck in misunderstanding and brokenness simply because we don't know what to do or what to say. *Mended* will give you a place to begin.

Sheila Walsh, author of *It's Okay Not to Be Okay*

The mother-daughter relationship is one of the most sacred and yet often one of the most complicated. In *Mended*, you'll find hope and the tools of conversation that you need to repair your broken relationship. Written beautifully and tenderly, this book is a must read. I highly recommend it!

Becky Harling, author of *How to Listen So People Will Talk*

Mended is a delicate yet powerful glimpse into the lives of two women who have done the hard work of restoration, producing a relationship characterized by bridges rather than walls. The practical insights they offer make their book as practical as it is poignant, a gift that mothers and daughters will cherish for generations to come.

John Hambrick, author of *Move Toward the Mess*

Mended

Blythe Daniel & Dr. Helen McIntosh

HARVEST HOUSE PUBLISHERS
EUGENE, OREGON

Cover design by Connie Gabbert Design + Illustration

Front cover: photos © Phatthanit, Ruslan Grechka / Shutterstock, Hand-lettering by Connie Gabbert Design + Illustration

---

Disclaimer
This book is not intended as a substitute for counseling or therapy. It is meant to encourage you in your relationship with your mother or daughter—to equip you with language, ideas, and principles to bring about needed repairs, growth, and healing.

Mended
Copyright © 2019 by Blythe Daniel and Helen McIntosh
Published by Harvest House Publishers
Eugene, Oregon 97408
www.harvesthousepublishers.com

ISBN 978-0-7369-7351-9 (Trade)
ISBN 978-0-7369-7352-6 (eBook)

Library of Congress Cataloging in Publication Data is on file at the Library of Congress, Washington, DC.

Printed in the United States of America
19 20 21 22 23 24 25 26 27 / BP-GL / 10 9 8 7 6 5 4 3 2 1

We dedicate this book to the mothers and daughters
before us and after in our family tree:

Emma Jean Bryan Brown

Maris

Calyn

Lynn

Sarah

Ann

And to the wonderful sons and fathers who stood with them:

James

Art

William

Bryan

May you always know how much we love your hearts
and how very dearly they have impacted ours!

Contents

Foreword

Stasi Eldredge

When I go to a mechanic, I go to one who absolutely loves being a mechanic. I want a person who has spent time under the hood, someone who has experience and expertise. If I need to go to anyone, really, for anything, I want that person to be passionate about his or her work. To be trustworthy. To be drawing upon a deep well of experience. To that end, if I want to learn about the relationship between a mother and daughter—the possibilities for healing, the goodness and holiness and intimacy that can be attained—I go to Blythe Daniel and Helen McIntosh. So you, lucky reader, are in the right place.

I've had the pleasure of being in the company of these two many times. Their mutual delight in one another, coupled with their mutual respect, is alluring. Both are fully themselves in each other's company, with no hint of the strained facial expressions prevalent in too many daughters in the presence of their mothers, and vice versa. In them, I don't see what I shared with my own mother for too many years before she passed, but I do see what can be possible. I also see what I want to know between myself and the daughters given to me through the marriages of my sons.

The mother-daughter relationship is a holy one. It can be marked by years fraught with the messy angst of needed separation. There can be seasons of appropriate or displaced anger. Certainly, there are many moments when emotions run high. And there is the other side too. The beauty of the shared experience of femininity. The knowing of navigating this life as a girl and then as a woman. The possibility of having an advocate in your mother through the transition from child to adult. The potential future of a deepening friendship built upon a shared history and a mutual love. I believe in her heart of hearts every mother longs to mother well. And every mother needs help doing it. I believe every daughter would love a healthy and life-giving relationship with her mother. And every daughter needs help with that too.

Which you already know and is probably what led you to pick up this book. Well done.

No matter where you are currently in your relationship with your mother or your daughter, there is hope for a better one. It may feel impossible, but nothing is impossible for our God.

When Gabriel told Mary she was to bear the Son of God, she asked, "How will this be?" and the angel told her, "Nothing will be impossible with God" (Luke 1:37). And when the disciples asked, "Who then can be saved?" Jesus said, "The things that are impossible with people are possible with God" (Luke 18:26-27). Ecclesiastes 9:4 says, "Where there's life there is hope," but with God, there is hope even when there appears to be no life at all (Ezekiel 37). There is hope for your relationship, dear one, and nothing is out of the realm of possibility for our Jesus.

Because of Jesus, we don't have to live this life alone or figure out how to live it well all by ourselves. We have a Guide. We have a Helper. We have a Counselor. We have one another. And now we have this book.

Blythe and Helen possess a shared wisdom won by plumbing the depths of God's heart in the good seasons and the hard. They share what they have learned with a winsome, wise, and generous hand. This book is filled with tangible counsel written by women who follow hard after Jesus and who, with compassionate hearts, understand the struggles we all face.

Mended is an invitation to follow Jesus into the heart realms of desire, brokenness, hope, and healing. It is a journey worth taking, and one on which God will guide you with gentleness and mercy. Ultimately, this book is a call to love. It is a call we are all meant to answer.

God bless you as you do. Such goodness awaits.

Introduction

Blythe

We were just a few days into summer break and catching our breath from all the end-of-school excitement. The pace of the slower days was so appealing to both me and my children. We had started to dream about what the summer would hold, days when we could get away from the tasks that persistently called our names for attention. The phone rang, and when I cheerfully answered the call, her words gripped me in ways I didn't have a response to. I heard the words "may have lymphoma," and I couldn't connect the sentence with the person who was saying it.

I had spent time with Mom the week prior, and there was nothing in her appearance or words then that would have made me think something new was about to impact her life and our family. She always had a healthy glow, a spirit that filled a room, a heart that—unlike the Grinch's, which was two sizes two small—was three times a normal size, I was convinced.

In the moments that followed, there were words and feelings that seemed suspended in the ceiling above me. I had a difficult time processing what I'd just heard. No! We were writing a book together; we had so many things to do this year. This was not something that was on my radar *at all* that would be a part of my story with my mom. Thankfully, I didn't then, or in the days after, go to a place of "Why my mom?" For we don't really get to ask that question, do we?

I do remember asking a few questions of Mom and Dad about how and when they would know for sure—and then I prayed with them. I remember holding back tears so as not to cave in to the dark thoughts that wanted to take over. In that moment, what mattered most was that Mom would continue to know life and I would know life with her.

Mothers and daughters. There is something about the way we feel toward each other. Many mothers and daughters can sense the chasm between them. Maybe that's why you picked up this book. We're so glad you are thinking about your relationship with your mother or daughter.

In a sense, I felt a chasm occur the moment Mom shared with me that she wasn't healthy. It was as if something huge divided us—her health and the future in front of us.

While our love was intact (we had worked hard to get it there), there was something we had to address between us that now called us deeper to each other. And it was a matter of choosing life over the darkness of walking into an unknown path with each other.

Some daughters have not experienced the feeling of "What if I lose my mom?" with the sense that life would alter dramatically for them in a negative way. Some mothers and daughters, and maybe you are one of them, have felt they have already lost their daughter or mom in their relationship, and they live each day with the chasm in their hearts. They wonder if they will ever gain her back.

And then there are daughters and mothers who have wondered, *What if my daughter never calls me again? What if my mom doesn't want to come see my family? How will I feel if I never get to repair the relationship I have with my mom?*

This is the purpose of our book. It's to ask these hard questions and address them with hopeful expectation for you. No mom or daughter wants to walk a dark path of uncertainty, a strained relationship, or a gulf between you that feels too difficult for you to cross.

The most beautiful and the most volatile relationships are often between a mother and daughter. Why is that? We believe it is because we are formed in our mother's womb and we are carried by our moms to give us life (and not just life inside the womb but also *for* life, meaning over the years). This bond can either impact us for the better or leave us hurting pretty deeply. Many daughters do not feel accepted or even wanted. And that is something we will address in this book since it's part of our story as well. Forgiveness is one of the biggest issues between a mother and daughter, and bitterness can grow when one or both are expecting the other to ask for forgiveness and they can't let go.

One thing we want to get out right up front: You are loved by God and you have purpose and worth. God formed you and fashioned you, and you have great value:

> You created my inmost being;
> you knit me together in my mother's womb.
> I praise you because I am fearfully and wonderfully
> made (Psalm 139:13-14 NIV).

You may have a rocky relationship with your mom or daughter. But it does not mean you are any less loved and valued because of it.

And two, there is no fear or shame you need to carry in your life. None. Zip. We bear the souls of our Maker. And in Him, there is only love and acceptance. There is no shame or fear.

A couple of months before the phone call with Mom about her diagnosis of lymphoma, which brought my relationship with her in sharper focus, my pastor shared these words: "God will take you into the cave you fear most to show you there's nothing to fear." And I truly felt no fear during the entire season that followed with Mom. I let go of fear's power over me, and that's what we do when the enemy of our souls, Satan, tries to bring a judgment on us that's not ours to take.

As mother and daughter, we see what we mean to each other more clearly now. We look for the signs of our relationship with more eagerness than before. We see how God shows us the truths that point to His good character even in harder times, and we know He sees us in our relationship as mom and daughter and He is visible to us. And the same is true of you and your mother or daughter. He does not leave where He is asked to dwell.

God provided instruction for all relationships through one of the wisest men who ever lived: King Solomon. His words in Proverbs 20:7 are, "The righteous lead blameless lives; blessed are their children after them" (NIV), and verse 11 says, "Even small children are known by their actions, so is their conduct really pure and right?" (NIV). The passage goes on in verse 20 to say, "If someone curses their father or mother, their lamp will be snuffed out in pitch darkness" (NIV) and verse 22: "Do not say, 'I'll pay you back for this wrong!' Wait for the LORD, and he will avenge you" (NIV).

That's some pretty strong language about how we are to look at our individual actions toward our father and mother and even our children. Are our actions to each other out of a pure motive? Verse 7 says the righteous one who leads a blameless life has blessed children after him. We aren't blameless, but we are righteous in Christ! It's clear in this passage and in other verses in Proverbs that man's steps should be directed by the Lord, and when we try to activate our own justice, we are attempting to short-circuit God. Throughout Proverbs the author frames wisdom and understanding over hasty decisions, trying to acquire the wrong things, and pride. All of these affect our relationship with our mom and/or daughter.

Here's the good news. God knows our hearts (He made us, right?), and He is strengthening them in every relationship we have if we let Him. He knows what you are up against, and He wants you to have the tools to honor your mom or daughter and live wisely with her. The Lord can and will deliver you both!

As mother and daughter, we hope there is nothing to fear in your relationship with your mom or daughter, but if there is, peace can be experienced now, not just on some future day when you hope to be reunited. Restoring what God created between you is what we want to offer you. Mothers and daughters are often linked in our culture in both positive and negative ways. When women think about who they are, it's possible they think about how they are similar to their mother or how they don't want to be like her at all. But no matter where your paths have taken you, there is a path you can both take to bring yourselves back to each other. Yes, now. Not later, but now.

The Bible has a lot to say about restoring relationships. We believe God's design is for families to pursue Him even when their families are messed up. And messed up they are!

The book of Isaiah has become a favorite passage for both of us. Mom introduced me to its life-giving words before I could memorize them for myself. She pointed out to me the foundation for the words we will share with you. Her favorite words, which she has taught me and my children, are *rebuild*, *restore*, and *repair*. Notice how they come up in these two passages:

Isaiah 58:12: "Those from among you will *rebuild* the ancient ruins; you will raise up the age-old foundations; and you will be called the *repairer* of the breach, the *restorer* of the streets in which to dwell" (emphasis added).

Isaiah 61:4: "Then they will *rebuild* the ancient ruins, they will raise up the former devastations; and they will *repair* the ruined cities, the desolations of many generations" (emphasis added).

Rebuild, yes. Repair, check. Restore, yes. Don't these words speak life to you?

Is your heart longing to mend or make better part of your relationship with your mother or your daughter? Maybe you are a mentor of spiritual daughters and you want to show them a picture of what mothers and daughters can look like. Perhaps you are a daughter without a mentor or a mom you can say was a good role model, and you desperately want to get it right with your daughter. Or perhaps you are a mom who wants to get it right with your daughter before life takes you too far apart from each other. You want to experience the goodness a mother and daughter can have and operate more freely in your homes and with each other.

And we know operating in our homes with each other brings our relationships into full light, doesn't it?

Many of us walk in the authority of our own home as mothers. Some daughters are not yet mothers but long to be so they can do things differently than they experienced. They want to *rebuild*. Rebuilding what you want to have with your mother or daughter is a gift worth seeking. In fractured times with your family, specifically with a mother or daughter, you want to be able to *repair* what's between you. We get it! We know there are mothers and daughters who have broken dreams, broken conversations, and broken relationships that need repair. We have done that too.

Women have the heart to help mend. Traditionally that's been their role. They're the ones to speak the hard things that have not yet been said and to quiet the disturbing words going back and forth between children. Women know how to mend their children's scrapes and deal with the illnesses of a parent, but why do they feel so inadequate to mend hearts between mothers and daughters?

So many mothers have abandoned their role. There is a splintered modeling of mothering. This is where the *restorer* comes in. The restorer is the one who seeks to bring life out of the ruins. To restore means not to ignore but to choose to make things new. Restoration: to give you the gift of mothering and of being mothered.

Restoring the heart is a spiritual journey. As you go to God, He restores you, and you gain a restored heart. The heart before God is key to the heart before your mother or daughter. If your heart is not fully toward God, it will be difficult to navigate the relationship with your mother or daughter.

We understand that sometimes it can feel as though God could have changed things between you, and it's difficult to recognize God as a restorer. We can often build walls around our hearts toward God and toward our mother or daughter. But these walls won't edify us—they often will destroy us. We know ancient cities had walls to fortify them. The city was the metropolis that needed protecting, and often a city had many villages. Walls were meant to keep out the enemy. But the walls we build between a mother and daughter don't hold back an enemy—they hold back a relationship.

In this book we want to help you awaken your heart to God as the restorer of all things, including your relationships. We want to show you how to build bridges between a mother and daughter, not walls.

Bridges allow you to gain entry to an area—you can walk from one side to the other without interference. A mother and a daughter may not walk completely to the other's side (although our hope is that they would!), but they can walk closer toward each other and meet in the middle.

Jesus was the ultimate bridge builder. He bridged relationships with mothers, daughters, fathers, and sons through His words, His healing touch, and His interactions with them. The prophet Isaiah looked at the generation before him and at the ruins that were rebuilt and proclaimed to the people how their refusal of God and His covenants kept them in captivity by the Babylonians. And he foretold of the coming King Jesus, who would ultimately be the bridge builder between all the not-so-good things we've done in our lives—known as sin—and a just God.

All those who are willing to stand in the breach (Isaiah 58:12) and become willing to repair their own life and then help rebuild the relationship with their mother or daughter will experience new life that comes from restoring, repairing, and rebuilding.

Women have gotten lost in their roles as mothers and daughters, sometimes not knowing what to say or do. And they particularly don't know what to do when they see or experience brokenness.

How do you mend a broken heart or a broken relationship? The culture doesn't have the answer, but we want to give you the tools you need to navigate the relationship with your mother or daughter that has caused you pain and maybe even threatened to pull you apart.

This book will help you become a better mother or daughter, and we will share with you how you can reclaim the role you want to have as a mother or daughter. Many mothers don't know how to be a mother who is both strong and sensitive, and they don't have a role model of healthy mothering. We often hear mothers and daughters acknowledge that their relationship is not what they want it to be or thought it would be. But we believe daughters can learn to mother their children and have a relationship with their mother that is exceedingly better than what we see or hear from mothers and daughters today.

We are built for relationships with each other. And when there has been a chasm or there seems to be difficulty even talking with one another without defensiveness or hurt, it hurts more than just the two of you. Generations are affected by how you and your mother or daughter relate and interact with each other. And if the relationship doesn't even exist anymore, further hurt can divide families. As a first step, we invite you to acknowledge that you want a different future. Don't focus on how yet. Just tell God you want to make things better between you and you need His power to do so.

He has done that for our family and the generations represented in our family. And we know He can do that for you as you trust Him even with a small seed of faith. It's not up to us to fix a person—only Jesus Christ can do that. But we can move toward restoring what's been lost because He specializes in that for us and will give us what we need to do this well.

And we invite you to dream with us about what your relationship can be restored to and how this will impact your family and generations to come. You hold a powerful tool—the words that can bring life—and those words are needed more now than ever. It's your season to rebuild and repair, and we are expectant and hopeful with you about what this can look like. Let's jump in together!

I See You, You See Me: The Layering of Us

Blythe

Our family loves chocolate. A more perfect food than this delicious taste of heaven does not exist. So when my daughter Calyn was seven, she asked me if she could put chocolate milk in her cereal. I paused. Bit my lip. Because who wouldn't want chocolate milk in her cereal? I quickly thought, *More sugar, less nutritious than white milk...Hmm...Probably not.* With that, I told her, "No, honey, you can't have chocolate milk in your cereal." Her mind is constantly processing ideas and good comebacks. I'm told she is a lot like me at that age, and I'm not one to argue with truth.

So using her quick wit and memory, she came back with, "Nannie puts it in her cereal. Did you know that?" Wait, what? How did she remember that? She'd cracked our code of chocolateness. And she came back with an argument I didn't even know how to respond to. My girl had gotten me.

Four months earlier, my mom and dad had come to visit us. One morning, as is typical in our bustling household, we didn't have enough white milk (do you know how often I go to the grocery store? It's pretty much daily because we constantly run out of milk and other important things) so Mom used the chocolate milk we had in her cereal, and Calyn remembered that. She saw my mom. Then she looked at me.

She knows the common ground between us is chocolate. Her grandmother gives her a certain kind of chocolate treat each Christmas, and their love of chocolate is one of the things that bonds them together. I have sat on the couch with her eating M&Ms while we watched a movie. But life is more than chocolate, isn't it? I mean, it's a great part of life. But what's most important is finding the common ground between you and your mother, or you and your daughter or granddaughter. And at the heart of what you are building between you and your mother or daughter is this: I see you, and you see me.

But as we get older and words have been said between us as mothers and daughters and grandmothers, the chocolate melts and the things that held you together are no longer strong enough. Our hearts hurt as we think about the words or moments between us that have left us feeling like our relationship cannot be mended.

Maybe you feel like you've blown it with your daughter or mother and you wonder how to get back what you once had. Or maybe you never had the relationship you longed for and the wounds have created a scar in your heart that hasn't healed over time. She didn't stand up for you when you needed it. Her words hurt you. Her actions showed you anything but love. And when you tried to talk with her about it, the conversation escalated into an overwhelming argument. And it's still awkward today to spend time together. You don't know your place or how you can be in her presence without bringing up your hurt feelings and exploding.

And it may not even seem possible that you can have a relationship with your mother or daughter because of the life lived between you. You may be in a season where one of you has detached from the other and there is little hope of reconciling. Or there's been an offense so great you don't feel like your relationship can ever be restored.

There's the fact that she no longer calls. Or that you have cut off communication with her because of your anger, and silence has come between you. It could be she is no longer on this earth, and you want to reconcile your heart with what you have experienced as a mother or daughter but you don't know how to do that with someone who is gone. Or you have a sense that your relationship isn't how it could be or should be, and you are weary from carrying this load to yet another destination in your heart and closing her off from you or your children.

Relationships can become toxic with buried emotions and unspoken words. You might have to be the initiator of healing, and doing this for your heart will be worth it. Healing may take some time, and what we are about to suggest is not to make a quick gesture and then quickly scoot away (we do this when we aren't sure of the other's reaction, right?), but over a period of time we hope you will see this as a thread of investment in the other.

Find the common ground between you and celebrate it. We believe there is always at least one thing you can find that is common ground with your mother or daughter. It may be as trivial as chocolate. It may be a fun location you like to go to. It could be a food or a memory from school. But the key is to find it, to accentuate it, and to invest in it with her. Find something that can draw you together rather than tear apart the fabric between you.

This builds your relationship even if it is the only thing you have in common. Building your relationship is what can give you hope that you will move out of the season you have lived in pain, expecting that things would just stay the same and you would adjust and live life without the other person rather than live in fullness of the relationship you'd so dearly love to have. We want more than that for you, and if we had to guess, we believe you do too! In finding common ground, one of the things you are doing is sharing the individual thoughts and desires you both have in neutral territory. What comes next is putting the other first. Okay, exhale. There is great reward in this. Stay with us!

Putting the Relationship First

Blythe

If the bottom layer is finding common ground, the next layer is putting the relationship between you first. The relationship between you can be so much better, and learning ways to put the relationship first above the different interests or beliefs you have is key.

My mother didn't have the luxury of a lot of great, shared moments with her mother. My grandmother was battling the effects of anger, alcoholism, and anxiety that were present due to her mother's choices of how she lived life. Her mom operated out of a brokenness that had come to her from a previous generation. And no one taught her mom how to fight for the things she loved rather than fall into the trap of past sins and heartbreak.

Mom had to help run a household, take care of a sick mom, care for the needs of her younger brother, and help her dad who was a busy air force commander. The family moved a lot and was often in places that family couldn't get to them and come to the aide of my mom. I often marvel at what she was doing at nine years old when I look at my nine-year-old daughter now.

As painful as I can only imagine that was for my mom, I like to think there were things she and my grandmother had in common. And that my grandmother did love my mom and showed her as best she could in the brokenness she was living out of.

I do remember my grandmother loving to shop, and I have heard how she would take my mom to nice places to shop on occasion and let her enjoy a tasty treat at their favorite store. I imagine, based on what I know of what Mom heard as a young girl, it was probably accompanied by comments such as, "Are you sure you're wearing that?" "You look too plain," and other statements that were hurtful to a little girl just wanting to enjoy a day with her mom. But there was common ground.

As Mom got older, she put the relationship with her mother first rather than just focusing on the common ground. She looked at how she could come alongside and help her mom. And Mom has continued to live this way, putting the relationship first as a mom and grandmother, and she has done this well. She loves taking my children shopping. It is their thing, especially the girls. They look forward to it, and they revel in how she loves them and wants to give them good gifts. But this couldn't have come about just by simply doing life as she has always done it. Mom had to rebuild from what she experienced.

Living your present like you did your past is often limiting the joy and freedom that is yours through the work of Jesus Christ. We aren't supposed to just muscle through, but we receive the ability to love outside our own means by taking hold of what Jesus gives us—the ability to deeply care for another because of how He cares for us.

Somewhere along the way an intentional shift has to take place if you want to invest in your relationship with your mom or daughter and in future generations. It won't come without some choices to lay down what did or didn't happen, how it was expressed to you, and how it left you feeling.

Our good friend and wise woman Stasi Eldredge puts it this way:

> Not a one of us is a perfect mother, and none of us had one. God alone is perfect...The role of a mother is profound, and the role *your* mother has played and continues to play in your life is utterly central to shaping the woman you are today...As a woman, your mother is your most potent role model. How she felt, what she thought, and what she believed had a direct effect on you.[1]

God woke me up early today. I thought I heard pitter-patter, and my daughter Calyn had come into our room and made a little place for herself on the floor. I picked her up and put her in our bed. She said she couldn't sleep. I laid there kissing on her like my mom used to do on me. Mom intentionally set a pattern for caring for me this way, which I then repeated to my daughter. This goodness is possible because God has helped us *a lot* to love as He loves. Mom and I have let Him mend us personally and also mend any unraveling in the mother-daughter relationship over the years. Mom and I want you to know our story so that you will be deeply encouraged as we share not just successes but the many repairs that brought us here.

Helen

The driving force behind this book is to share that we believe "we can only do what we can do." You can only work on your own half of the relationship. We are not calling you to single-handedly repair or enrich your relationship with your mother or your daughter (the whole enchilada, as we say)…just your part! You are only responsible for your own words, actions, thoughts, hopes, and dreams.

You are not responsible for the other person or their issues, but we will share how those are clues in navigating the relationship. You are not responsible for the other party's response to you or to your efforts. When the subject of responsibility comes up, I almost always think of the visual of two cups bumping, with a picture of a heart drawn on each cup and numerous arrows spilling out of each cup. The heart, of course, represents our individual heart. The arrows represent the "issues" of our lives that spill from our heart, as shown in Proverbs 4:23: "Watch over your heart with all diligence, for from it flow the springs of life." I like to replace the word *springs* with *issues* because that's what comes up and out. We are responsible for bumping someone's cup by what we say or do, but not for what comes out of their cup. But we are very responsible for what comes out of our own cups/hearts!

Should your mom or daughter not respond well because of a relational mistake you have made, I will discuss some ways you can own it and do damage control. The focus is on your heart, your words, your actions, and your choices. I hope you have just said to yourself,

"Whew!" and your shoulders are more relaxed. We are not asking you to climb a mountain in the dead of winter with no equipment.

Along with continually asking yourself, "What am I responsible for, and what am I *not* responsible for in a difficult relationship?" it is helpful to think of the mother-daughter relationship as a living organism. You may ask yourself, "What do I need to do to pour into this relationship?" "What needs protecting?" "What needs shoring up?" "What do I build into the relationship today?" "What do I need to do to make things better?" And then the most intentional question of all: "What do I need to do to better honor my mother/daughter, whether deserved or not?" Could it be an investment of unconditional love? Does that sound like the way God treats us? Let's look at this more closely.

How Can You Help?

Do you ever feel like trying to help might hinder or make things harder in your relationship with your mother or daughter? Perhaps instead of trying to do many things, you can focus on finding common ground, putting the other person first, and investing in the relationship. There are three specific things you can do to help improve your relationship with your mother or daughter:

1. Invest in your relationship with God.
2. Pray for your mom or daughter.
3. Plan something for your mom or daughter that doesn't require more of you than you can offer.

These things will put equity in your own bank and in the other person's—even if they don't respond the way you hope they will. It will be healing for your heart to do these things so that you know you have done all you can do and are not living in the land of "I could have tried something different" or "I'm not sure if I've done my part." We want you to be equipped to do what you know you can do and not have room for any regrets.

Blythe

Let's dive into these more closely. First, investing in your relationship may be an investment of seeing your daughter or mother more. It might mean making a sacrifice to drive to see them or an investment of time to Facetime or Skype with them or use a video conferencing service. If you live close, it might be suggesting you want to do something for her while she is at work (because you both have a job and you know how much this would mean to you in reverse), or you could offer to help with a specific chore or prepare some food while she is there, and it would provide a time for you to talk while an activity is going on. If these things aren't an option, perhaps your investment would be something you can provide to meet a need and show her you care about her. It might be a monthly subscription service for meals, a vitamin or supplement plan you pay for, a laundry service, or a babysitter to come once a week. But whatever it is, you want her to see how you are invested in her. My mom has done this in practical and helpful ways. She sends us restaurant gift cards so we can enjoy a night out, and she sent us supplements when the kids were young because she wanted us to be able to ward off sickness since we were picking up germs about as often as I picked up their toys!

One way I made a relational investment with my daughter Maris was by coming to her class to talk about how to get a book published since that is part of my job. She raised her hand with an answer almost each time I asked the class a question. Her shy spirit came flooding open with words and responses when I was there. I hope she saw my presence as an investment of time. Hopefully I can continue to find ways to build into my daughters the truth that I want to be a part of what they do and bridge my world to theirs.

Second, pray for your mom or daughter. This sounds matter-of-fact, but it's so important. One of the things I remember about my mom when I was growing up was that she prayed for us each day before school. And that has continued. She prays for me every day and often sends me a text reminding me of what she is praying for that day.

We can't take this for granted. We need to grab hold of the need to pray for one another and make it a priority. Even if you don't know how to pray or what to pray for the other, holding her up to the Lord is one of the greatest blessings you can offer. I have heard, and I bet you have too, of people who felt they were beyond receiving prayer. But the other kept on praying and things shifted, and they are a different person today because of prayer! Let us be women who pray more often than we complain or try to figure things out on our own. Prayer is important to us and to God. Help from heaven shifts things for us on earth!

And third, plan something for you and your mother or daughter that doesn't require more of you than you can give. Plan for where you are, not where you want to be. It might be a simple outing to return something to a store and grab coffee near the store. It might be a shared activity that allows you to spend a brief time together. Don't feel guilty if you aren't ready for an all-day shopping trip. Be where you are and who you are. Time will help overcome obstacles as you talk more freely, and we want to help you know what to say in these times together.

So what follows in these pages is a menu of ideas, prayers, and principles that can repair generations of poor patterns, shatter years of bad memories, and make things new for the present and future. The fact that you have chosen to read this book, to invite us into your life, is something we value tremendously. We hope you see transformations in the fragmented places of your heart and mind.

Mending Thread

What concerns do you have with your mom or daughter? What's difficult in your relationship or what are the things you don't feel comfortable talking about? What is the difficulty and how would you like it to be restored?

Focus on looking up at what God is doing in your relationship as you pour into and invest in your relationship. What does the common ground between you look like? It's a new day. We want you to see this as a new beginning.

> Behold, I will do something new,
> Now it will spring forth;
> Will you not be aware of it?
> I will even make a roadway in the wilderness,
> Rivers in the desert (Isaiah 43:19).

What is the new thing you would like to see God do in your relationship?

When you are tempted to think you continually live in the old ways and old patterns with your mom or daughter, either journal or write out your thoughts on your phone—anywhere you can see it, write what God is doing in your life and in your relationship with your mother or daughter that is *new*. Remember what these good moments feel like so you can repeat them again and again. As you see the fruit of your efforts, be sure to share with your mother or daughter at least one thing God is doing that is producing something new between you. It will encourage you both!

Making It Personal: Craft a Phrase

Blythe

We'd like to invite you to either paint, scrapbook, or craft something that could show a phrase you want to adopt for yourself. My younger daughter said some words of encouragement to me when I told her I wasn't sure how I was going to do something I needed to do with Mom. She said, "Just go with it. You've got this." I love that and have made those words mine. They are a reminder of what I want to see happen in our relationship.

What is the phrase you want to place as a mantle over your

relationship? It should be something that prompts you to think about putting your mom or daughter first. Something that causes you to think of and really *see* them before focusing on yourself.

Use this as an opportunity to tap into your creativity to make something that will be a reminder to you of what you are investing in and, each time you see it, will say to you, *My investment is worth it.*

It may be a piece of artwork that you later share with your mother or daughter. We often love what our daughters or our mothers make. What can you gain by creating something with her? A chance to build a bridge closer to her. Restoring through creating. You've got this!

2

Being Right or Being Closer: Relationship Above Differences

Helen

When I was growing up, I wanted to be closer to Mom. She wanted to be right. Our times together in the kitchen weren't plentiful, but they were often painful. I remember wanting to be with Mom in hopes that something could bring us closer together and something I could do would please her. But often it would seem like failure would crush these waves of hope, and I wasn't sure why our relationship couldn't be what I imagined it could be between us.

I remember washing lettuce was something I tried to do to help my mom and show her I wanted to please her. But it never worked out as I hoped, and instead of bringing us together it would tear us apart. She would rage at the way I washed lettuce, which caused me to wonder how we could be so different that I couldn't even wash lettuce correctly. Almost every time I tried to help her I didn't do it "right," and her response took the wind out of my sails every time. I kept going back to the kitchen and the lettuce washing thinking the next time she wouldn't explode. But her anger always surfaced. It seemed to me that Mom cared more about being right than how we related to each other.

We all desire to be noticed and loved, but those needs are more pronounced in families where there are big differences in how members relate to each other. Each person wants to be their own individual and express who they are. But this desire can work negatively against us when there is disharmony in our relationships. And it made me doubt myself rather than feel accepted for who I was because of the way my mom saw me.

In this chapter we want to explore the feelings behind putting the relationship ahead of differences. One way of addressing our differences is isolating; another is freeing. How do you want to be known in your relationship with your mother or daughter?

Often we let our differences of opinions get in the way of our relationship with our mother or daughter. We have to let those go and put the relationship ahead of our differences, even if it means not trying to prove we are right. Releasing your need to be right in order to reconnect to your mother or daughter is key, and we want to share ways to help this happen.

When we say differences of opinion, that could mean a variety of things, from differences of how to raise children, to differences on stances that affect your lifestyle and beliefs, or even differences of opinion of how life is "supposed" to be. Because my mom was dealing with illness, addiction, and personal issues that had nothing to do with me, and because of her inability to handle life in those days, our relationship was on rocky footing much of the time. She had issues with anxiety and anger, and she projected them onto me in many ways. Doing small tasks such as not washing lettuce the "right" way or not cutting up carrots her way were mainly when the explosions would happen. Even then I knew her rage wasn't really about lettuce and carrots.

Every time her anger would blast at me, I remember thinking I didn't want to lose the relationship in spite of the sharp differences we were experiencing in such basic routines. Sadly, I'm not sure I ever really spoke up to her—I didn't know how to at the time—but I remember thinking the overall relationship was more important than the incident at hand, even though I didn't want to minimize the conflict. I learned to see I did the best I could with what I had.

How We Handle What We Have

Helen

Sometimes we aren't sure how to react in a situation. Blythe and I want to share some tools to help you navigate the many different ways mothers and daughters view life and the enormity of the opinions attached to those variances of thinking. I regret that my mom and I weren't able to dialogue about our own differences. She didn't discuss things. It was either "her way or the highway." Some families discuss things better than others. I wish I could have owned that we weren't doing so well, but we weren't even healthy enough to have that conversation. I can say I did want the relationship more than I wanted to be right and I protected the relationship in spite of our differences of opinion. Though I wish I could have said, "I see your anger. Something is not going well for you. Can we talk about this? Can we agree that the relationship is more important than the way the lettuce was washed?"

Emptying the dishwasher was another dysfunctional danger zone. I seldom ever did that "right." Now I see her control issues came out in her opinions about how a kitchen should function. And it was not a happy place. I continued to go back into the battle zone to help her —and to hopefully help the relationship, but we both needed much more than kitchen help!

The good news is that every difficulty I had with my mom helped me in countless ways in my relationship with Blythe. I definitely learned not to be so critical of Blythe. My own mom had a critical spirit that suffocated me day by day. For the longest time I thought something terrible was wrong with me. I longed to let Blythe be who she was, and she has always been what I call "velvet steel"—soft on the outside in how she approaches people but strong and fiery on the inside. This has served her well, and I see her daughters repeating the pattern as well. She was often choosing her own path all the way through high school, and I tried not to say anything to stifle her independent spirit but instead let her be her own maturing young woman.

Blythe

In my last year of high school I really wanted to be on my own, and I didn't listen to my mom as much as I could have. I didn't include her in my life as I once had, and I wanted to be by myself or with friends to a greater degree. I can't say it was a good time. I was starting to figure out my differences and how I would live on my own when I left for college. My relationship with Mom was still there, but I perceived that we had more differences than we actually did. I felt ready to leave to start a new life of college and believed I didn't have as much in common with Mom anymore.

I didn't put our relationship at the forefront like I had in the past. Mom says that when I left for college, she released me because I had said, "I am feeling smothered." I don't recall the exact ways I shared this with Mom, but I knew she had said goodbye to my brother the previous year when he went to college and now she was saying goodbye to me. In the years that followed, I made choices on my own of what sorority to join, what major to focus on, what relationships to have. And I remember Mom supporting me in those decisions.

Probably the biggest test for us was not one particular decision but living apart in the day-to-day decisions, and when there were any differences of thought, we couldn't bring them up because I was away from home and experiencing life on my own. I felt too proud to ask for help, and so I continued to make decisions on my own, affecting both my health and my finances.

By Christmas of my freshman year, I had spent the balance we set for my bank account, and I had lost enough weight that my parents were concerned. We had discussions about what life was looking like for me and how I could resolve it. As much as I knew my mom and dad wanted to help me, they let me make these decisions for myself, which in hindsight is a great way to learn how strong your relationship is and how you reap the results of the choices you make, both good and hard. They offered input, but they let the relationship have a greater place than being right.

Helen

Letting go of your child when she leaves for college and lives apart from you for the first time is a sure way to test your belief in her and requires you to put your relationship ahead of any differences you have. One of my favorite relational sayings that might help you handle these differences is this: **"What I want is a good relationship, and you are more important to me than this problem/this difference of opinion/this snag."**

Whenever a problem springs up, my default thought is always, *The relationship comes first.* That sets a tone for any discussions of differences of opinions to follow. Maybe the other person is actually right or maybe you are, but it is always right to honor the relationship. And not because they earned or deserved it. Honoring doesn't mean she is perfect. Honoring your mother does not mean you stuff down all the pain. We still encourage people to work on the brokenness in a relationship because it is a personal issue and it involves reconciliation with the other person. Hopefully repair can be facilitated for you and your mother or daughter. We will detail this more in the pages ahead, but for now we want to say that the relational scale between you should lean more heavily in her direction than yours—you are making the relationship a priority rather than declaring victory in your differences.

If a discussion between you is going south, it may be wise and

protective to say, "**Our relationship is more important than our differences of opinion on what is right, so we might want to pause this discussion for now**." It's not cowardice; it's wisdom to protect and leave
the discussion there if need be. It's the "we can't unscramble the eggs"
principle, because once you say something, it becomes part of the conversation and you can't undo it.

A great thing to say and do if you feel pressure to respond but you
don't want to is to say, "**Please excuse me. I need to leave things here**,"
as you exit the conversation and the room. It's okay to extend a boundary to protect you, your relationship, and your message. Some land
mines are to be kept in the distance and not addressed until the relationship is stronger and healthier. I wish I had known I could walk
away.

You may want to either pause the conversation for the time or walk
away to allow space for anger to settle down before you say something
you might regret or wish you could retract later. I know it's hard to say
something that feels less than the words you want to use. Proverbs 15:1
reminds us, "A gentle answer turns away wrath, but a harsh word stirs
up anger" (NIV). Sometimes you might respond with a gentle, "**I don't
want to fight with you to be right**," and that is a way to put the relationship ahead of who wins the argument.

Putting space between you shouldn't be an excuse not to talk but
an invitation to come back to the conversation later when there's been
some time between you. Your perspective may change. Hers may or
may not. But you can model the way to be honest and genuinely okay
with yourself and with her by not clinging to a need to prove how you
are right and she is wrong, or trying to win an argument but lose the
relationship.

We need to put a check on our need to be right. And it can start
with your walking away and proactively coming back to her in order
to tell her that you choose to *see* her, that she is more important than
who is right. These words may take you some time to develop because

you've not said them before. Will you consider trying it out? If all you have done is argue, do you want to explore another way?

From cover to cover, Scripture shows that God values relationship more than anything. We should follow the same model, right?

How to Value Someone Not Seen

It's a lot easier to talk with someone and work things out when that person is someone you see or talk to on a semiregular basis. But suppose the other person is a prodigal mom or daughter who has chosen a different belief system and lifestyle than you might wish or agree with. Your mom may have left to start a new life with a man who is now your stepfather. Your daughter may have gone ahead and moved in with her boyfriend despite your pleadings with her. These actions have caused distance in your relationship and it is being tested. But if you can sincerely communicate that you choose a relationship with her above the clash of choices, you have left a lifeline for the future.

Some daughters feel in order to protect themselves they need to leave the relationship. But a more common situation is when a mother or daughter doesn't feel valued, appreciated, or understood. But as we have shown, it never truly gets better between you until you address it with each other, until you come back into each other's presence. Does this remind you of the son in the prodigal son parable in Luke 15:11-32? What is interesting is that the younger son thought he needed to earn his father's acceptance upon returning home after he squandered everything. He probably thought he had lost the relationship as well. But he decided to move toward his father and their relationship. He humbled himself and came home rather than trying to prove he was justified in what he did, which hadn't worked out in his favor, and his father acknowledged and blessed him. The relationship was more important than his choices. His father wasn't looking to see if he or his brother was right—he simply wanted a relationship with his estranged son. And so it should be with us.

God has made mothers and daughters to be in relationship with each other no matter what is between us. Differences of opinion aren't the final words. Differences can be defining terms of agreement between you if you let them. A difference of opinion can turn into an agreement when you look for what you can come together on. Mothers and daughters carry weighty opinions about what is best for each, how they live life, and what they expect of the other on issues such as the roles within the family, what's best for raising children these days, values held, and more. You can lose a relationship over these differences.

And it's usually not the actual thing you disagree over that needs addressing. It's typically something else in your relationship where there has been a rub and it's expressing itself as a difference of opinion. And truly, there may be differences you can mutually agree on so that you can move past them and not get stuck on the differences. An agreement in its simplest state can allow you to move toward the other person by not allowing your differences to keep you apart. For example, you could agree with your mother that you both want your children to make memories with their grandparents even though you are struggling with feeling hurt that you didn't get as much attention from your parents.

Let's go back to the prodigal for a moment because often we all could feel like we either have been or were on the receiving end of a prodigal relationship. What if the prodigal is your mom? You as the daughter can speak the same message to her: that your relationship is bigger than the differences and that you don't want to live with the distance or disagreements between you. You want to think it's possible for you to have peace with the other and not discord. Often daughters feel that because they are the younger ones in the relationship, the mother has more power or influence. But you are on equal playing fields and share the responsibility of mending your relationship.

I do realize that living out the message is the harder part. However, saying "I choose a relationship" to yourself first (and then to your mother or daughter) sets the stage for the follow-up. Every word matters, doesn't it?

So what do you say exactly? You'll want to consult God and ask Him for the best words to say. He will fine-tune what you are to communicate, but the basic message will be something like this: **"Despite our differences, I do choose/want to have a relationship with you. Our relationship is far more important than our differences to me. Maybe we can talk about ways for us to do this."** At this point, you may want to ask her what she would like to say before you dive in to your responses. The two-way sharing is a start. If it doesn't go well the first time you bring it up, let her know you plan to circle back to it at a later time and that you hope you both can come up with at least one issue to work on together.

You both need to agree on the one issue so that you have the relational investment from both sides. You both need to be willing to work on what "it" is. Even if you may be sacrificing more than you want, it is a step in the right direction.

Some of us need to set our expectations higher when it comes to our mother or daughter. Often we think, *This won't (or can't) happen*, but we need to expect more. This is the way God calls us to live. We are to live in hope and expectation and not to place words on others or expectations that are so low. God says, "For My thoughts are not your thoughts, nor are your ways My ways...For as the heavens are higher than the earth, so are My ways higher than your ways and My thoughts than your thoughts" (Isaiah 55:8-9).

Setting the bar higher means we don't just make the lowest offer we can think of to move toward each other. Why not go big and ask for something you think they may not go for, but what if they do? The mother-daughter dance should involve asking for more than you think is possible and believing the results will come from God, who provides a way for everyone to be reconciled. Why shouldn't we initiate twists and turns in a new direction? You'll never know what the outcome could be if you don't ask.

We can set a higher expectation of restoration no matter if we are the daughter or mother, and there likely isn't anyone for whom these steps wouldn't apply.

As a mother, you may be trying to win over not just your daughter but her family. What do you say to an adult daughter who has become estranged from your nuclear family because of her spouse's influence? You may wish to say, "**I want us to be repaired in our relationship. Would you and your spouse be willing to share with me what you need to hear from me—or what I need to do—for us to be restored? I wish to clear up any offenses on my part.**"

Your mouth may have just dropped! Are you thinking, *My offenses? They're the ones who have done the offending!* But here's God's beautiful way: We are to clear up our end of things always, and sometimes we get to go first. Who is in the stronger place to initiate forgiveness: the one who has erred 5 percent or 95 percent? Maybe we were only 5 percent wrong, but we can initiate peace—always. God is our example. He reconciled us to Him through His Son, Jesus, who paid for our lives through His death. His resurrection is the reason we can have restoration. He represents the long-loving, love-pervading Father of the prodigal. Looking, waiting to initiate love.

When relationships are poor there is such pain. We are definitely wired to have relationships and to have good ones. And when we hurt, good relationships help. Said another way: Dysfunctional relationships bring pain and functional relationships help heal the fractured places in us. God is all about relationships and uses relationships to bring us to Him, and to restore us to Him and to others. It's one of His best gifts!

We know you may not be friends with your mother or daughter

right now. It may be so strained you don't see this closeness with her. But we see how the relationship with a mother or daughter can be invested in over time like a good ally. Our prayer for you would be that you would look to experience this closeness with her that God desires for us to have and provides for us even when connectedness feels off in a distant land.

John 15:5 is the classic word picture showing the beauty and rest available in our relationship with God. It says, "I am the vine, you are the branches; he who abides in Me and I in him, he bears much fruit, for apart from Me you can do nothing." Our role is abiding in Him and bearing fruit as a result. When we are in this place, we are so much freer to pass this on to our mother or daughter. Abiding in God means we go to Him first before we say something to our mother or daughter. We run things past Him before we speak it to the other. When we say it out loud to Him, we can often tell how it's going to sound. Bearing fruit comes as a discipline of letting Him be our first line of defense before saying something to our mom or daughter that we might later feel remorseful about.

A branch doesn't try to become a vine. Each has a place. There's no struggle. No striving. This is such a beautiful picture of mothers and daughters—the fruitfulness of our relationship when each knows her value. That's the goal.

No one and no relationship is beyond hope. We can tell you of many mothers and daughters we've heard from over the years as we have shared our story. People say, "I wish I could have a relationship with my mom/daughter like that." And what we say to them and to you is, "You can! It's not too late." When deep and lasting healing takes place in the relationship, this sets the relationship on a course of freedom and unity you can't pull apart.

Guarding the Bond as Mother and Daughter
Our good friend LaTan shared the following with us from her

experience of being a mother and putting aside differences to make her relationship with her daughter the primary focus.

Perhaps it was my own fault for raising her to stick to her guns, stay true to her convictions, honor her decisions. How could I expect her to cower to my wants simply because I'm her mother? But cower was exactly what I hoped for.

Taking another sip of my coffee helped ease the sudden, awkward silence after I'd expressed my opinions of why she shouldn't marry him. The look in her eyes told me her mind was made up. I knew that look. I have it too. And just like that, the sweetest memories of her childhood crashed over my rocky emotions. And then hot, salty tears fell like rain. A full-on ugly momma cry was in the forecast. The kind that starts in a momma's toes and moves, with tsunami force, through the core of her being after coming to grips with the reality that there will be no happily-ever-afters—not in this difference of opinion. Like an old movie reel, memories of her tiny feet secured inside the palms of my hands and the many prayers I'd prayed while caressing them, ever so softly, mocked me. "Lord, bless my sweet little girl. Fill her with wisdom. Give her faith-feet that guide her life to goodness."

Now that we are on the other side, I can say with confidence: Goodness even comes out of hardships. But letting go of our children hurts when what we are letting them go to is not God's best. There comes a time when our daughters must map their own life course, good or bad. Both mother and daughter must choose to navigate this transition carefully, letting go of guilt, condemnation, and blame.

It's important to put our differences aside, no matter how life-altering. Nothing matters more than fiercely guarding the bond of mother and daughter or fighting fiercely to cultivate brand-new bonds of love.

People come and go, but a mother-daughter bond is for a lifetime. Never allow any person or their poison to hinder mother-daughter closeness. Because if you were right, the truth will be revealed in time. And if you were wrong, you will be able to celebrate how you considered *her* feelings and honored your own opinion by expressing it but not allowing it to sabotage your relationship.

My daughter and I learned that even hard conversations can shape us into better people. Moms see the core of their children. Words that seem harsh can be the most powerful words with the most potential to cultivate growth. Expressing the hard things, while choosing respect over stubborn pride, proved powerful. Like throwing a rope across the great divide of our differences, we closed the gap by putting love for each other ahead of our differences of opinions. Later, when life hit the wall, our bridge was securely in place. We learned how, sometimes, it hurts to be right as much as it hurts to be wrong.

Today, we are closer, stronger, wiser because we made the decision to put our relationship ahead of differences of opinions.

Blythe

How do you see your ability to put your relationship ahead of your differences? I had the opportunity to put this into practice with my older daughter, Maris, on a particular occasion I remember well. Ironically, we were about to celebrate Valentine's Day—a day of love. We were expecting guests that evening. As I was cleaning up the house, I heard tears and then the pounding of footsteps on the stairs as my girls came to find me. After trying to find out what they had argued about, I asked them each to write down an account of what had happened. My younger daughter, Calyn, immediately set to work. Maris, however, was still trying to share with me what had occurred and why it wasn't all her fault. She was resistant to the assignment I had given them. I had seen some behaviors in the weeks preceding this that also caused me concern, but I knew only to address what was happening in the moment. Trying to deal with more at this time was not going to help; in fact, it would probably create a reaction of feeling like I piled a weight on her she couldn't or didn't need to carry.

We had a difference of opinion about how to move forward. And the more I pushed to show how "right" I was in making the declarations I did, the more she crumbled. What she needed was not for me to be right but to love her. I wanted to do the "right thing" by my discipline choice. She wanted to be loved. I have to tell you I didn't handle it well with her because I wanted justice. I wanted to move on before our guests arrived. And my need to have the situation wrapped up by the time our company came left Maris with red eyes and unresolved tears that she left on her pillow in hope that I would meet her there. Resolution came—later. But not as I would have wished.

Later, as I processed this with Mom, she made a good observation. She shared that Maris likes to be helpful. Maris's words to her sister that had led to Calyn's tears and their coming to find me in the first place were words to help her, but it didn't feel like help to Calyn—it felt like Maris was criticizing. And as I noticed this, I thought, *Maris was frustrated that she didn't get to help or fix the situation.* And in my need to show her I was right in disciplining her, I missed the need she had showed, which was to be able to share what she'd learned to help her sister. I learned, too, that my need to do the right thing as a mom isn't more important than our need to connect. I needed to show Maris ways to assist her sister with a loving but nonjudgmental spirit. It wasn't her job to teach but to encourage.

It was a humbling moment, but thankfully, I get to start over each day. No wonder I am a morning person! The promise of a new day and a fresh start in the morning excites me. And I get to figure out just how to put our relationship ahead of our differences.

The order of things is so important. I've noticed the yards I like best in our neighborhood are the ones where shiny, smooth stones are cemented and lined up, leading to a clear path toward the door of a home. I wonder what could be said of the stones, or words, I leave leading to the door of my daughters' hearts. There's the common saying about how stones may hurt us but words will not. We know this has often been said to show someone's strength, but inside we're crumbling at words spoken over us.

Stones are prevalent in the Bible. Listen to this perspective on stones: "In some places in scripture, a stone is used to describe strength and resiliency in a person's character. In the case of Peter before Christ's death, Jesus announces his new name will have the same meaning as a stone after Christ's death. This is to indicate the steadfastness and resolute nature that Peter will possess."[1]

What if we looked at the character we are building in ourselves and put a label on a stone of who we want to be or what we want to see in our life? A name that resembles the strength we want to have and the resiliency we long for in our relationship with our mother or daughter. I was at a writers conference where we took a stone and wrote something on it to depict what we wanted to acknowledge of God. On my stone, which sits on my desk, I wrote the word *Waymaker*. God is a waymaker, and He has made the way for me with my mom, and He can do the same for you with your mom or daughter.

It only takes one small stone to start a change. Even when it seems as though one stone of a good decision is a lonely start, the pile-up of good decisions or stones, one after another, builds a road to the other's heart that can't be achieved any other way.

I build this road with my girls every day, setting stone after stone. I picture the stones engraved with words like *mercy, intentionality, refresh, love unconditionally*—just like words are imprinted on Valentine conversation hearts. But these are stones on which our relationship rests. They remind me to lay down whatever is keeping us apart—my pride, my anger, my desire to be right—and pick up that which will help our relationship instead.

Mending Thread

Some of us are good at holding words close to our hearts and sharing them at just the right moment. Others of us need to process our words a bit before we react.

Do you know which kind of person you are? How will knowing this make a difference in how you react to your mother or daughter?

Do you need to verbally process in a quiet place with God before you share words with your daughter or mother? Are you one who needs to make some notes to come back to? Making notes to yourself that prompt you on what you were feeling and how you said you would handle it the next time you could see or talk with your mom or daughter can be very helpful. You may want to journal your thoughts to come back to as a reference. Or you may want to make notes in your phone before you text her. The notes can give you words when you don't recall your thoughts or don't know exactly what to say.

Differences of opinion are inherent and are normal and natural between mothers and daughters, but navigating them well requires some work. You may want to think about some new ways of responding when you have a difference of opinion with your mother or daughter. When you tend to respond in the ways you have in the past, the other person doesn't see you moving toward them. It doesn't seem like a genuine change is the goal.

If you are going to put the relationship first, you will probably need to humble yourself in the ways you approach things and be ready to admit your errors. You will want to make sure you are not trying to defend yourself but are instead extending yourself to the other. This requires thinking about what the other needs, not what you're comfortable giving.

Maybe your daughter or mother has not been truthful with you. And instead of calling them out on everything you see, you decide to focus on how to move forward rather than point out all the ways they let you down. You are living from a higher level, and you bring her up with you; you do not come down to the level of hurt. Bringing the other up to your level in how you share your words really is the best way to show you desire relationship over being right.

Making It Personal: Calling on Commonalities

Far too often we focus on our differences rather than what we have in common. We suggest you make a list of what you have in common. This might start with the reality that you both like to be right. But go beyond that. Think about things you both like, are proficient in, have done together, and can see commonalities in.

Ask your mother or daughter to do the same. Then compare your lists. We think you'll find that you have more in common to focus on than your differences.

If having a meal together is too complicated, if you might argue about where to go and when and what to eat, why not get together during your daughter's or your grandchildren's sporting or school events? If you are having the conversation too often about who is right when it comes to how best to host or whose turn it is, then avoid it by gathering at the event and either bypass eating together or do something else after. Gather on neutral territory and know where the land mines are. Don't put yourself in situations where you're trying to show that your opinion or your decisions matter most. Can you let go of the luxury of being right in order for peace to prevail? When you see the conversation is headed into toxic territory, can you steer it back to areas of agreement? We think you will see more of the areas of commonalities you may have forgotten or not talked about in a while, and this can help you raise your relationship to a new level.

Ready to make your list? Try to have some fun with it and see what might surprise you!

3

Saying What When: Words to Love and Live By

Helen

The inevitable "What do I say to my kids?" would happen when my children would misbehave. Blythe and her brother, Bryan, would often get into some mischief when I would need to focus on someone else or be out in public with them, and I remember feeling totally helpless to figure out how to react. I was desperate for answers. *What do I do? What do I say? How do I fix this?* It was a wake-up call that I didn't know how to discipline my children.

When Bryan was about three years old and Blythe was two, I had a deer-in-the-headlights season. I realized I knew nothing about how to discipline them. Every trip to the grocery store was a disaster, and every phone call to our home seemed to be an invitation for them to spring into actions they knew were wrong. I realized I was desperate to know what to do. I was a new Christian, but I knew enough to be sure that God would have something to say about raising children. My place of desperation on my knees became a place of security in my pouring through scriptures where I found insight from Him about how to parent.

Some have asked how I was able to pursue healthy mothering despite the unhealthy patterns surrounding me. The answer really is Jesus! I searched the Bible for a biblical way to be a mother. He gave me insights and direction and a great longing to learn how to be a good mother. And He provided many opportunities to grow in that. Bible studies and graduate studies gave many good ideas, but it was His unseen hand that helped me navigate the longing of my heart to be a healthy mother.

Often when I didn't know what to do or how to answer my children, I would pray. And I would mark these prayers in my Bible. I can still see where I prayed for my children for their decisions or things they needed help with and dates next to answers to prayers. Prayer has been a lifeline for me, and reading what God has to say has helped me align my thoughts and words with His.

As my children grew, I grew. And I learned what would resonate with them that I had never had the chance to have a mother ask me about. We grew together, and I think that perspective helped me and them see I didn't have all the answers.

Help to Know What to Say

Helen

Sometimes mothers and daughters don't know what to say to each other when there have been hurt feelings, time or space, or something more serious between you. *What do you say, exactly?* I have spent many years as a counselor, and I'll give some practical examples of what you can say—or *not* say—to minimize what you've been through and to encourage a better relationship between you. But part of my heart toward you is also from my own pain of experiencing this dilemma of not knowing how to address my own mom and the things between us.

I didn't know what to say to my mom much of the time. Sometimes I didn't address things, not because I didn't think they were important, but that was just my response. I didn't really see what was going on in me until Bryan, and then a year later Blythe, went to college. I knew things had been difficult, but I wasn't connecting the dots as an adult. When Blythe left, I saw my codependent issues. I had normalized everything when Bryan and Blythe were little. But when they left, I realized the issues in our family were serious because I was so profoundly sad and experienced a deep sense of loss. They were such a joy and comfort to me. And now there was a change of my role of care as a parent.

When my children came along, I didn't know how to parent because I had not been taught. All the way through their teen years, I did the best I could with God's help. But once they went to college, I had to begin to take a hard look at my issues, and I knew I had to choose to change my relationship with my mom. I knew our relationship wasn't healthy. Even though I'm not able to speak with her today because she's no longer alive, I would probably say something like this to her: **"Mom, I want us to do well. We've hit a hard place again, and I'm not sure what to say."**

I want to encourage you to speak. Admit there's a problem and you don't know what to say about it. What's valuable and important is that you're talking about "it," even if you are only admitting to the other person you don't know what to say. It's very humbling.

Hindsight is 20/20, but if I can help you be bold enough to say these hard things now, this is a good thing, and one that gets you on the right path to talk with your mother or daughter.

I was mute with my mother, but that was the only way I knew to be at the time. I wish I had asked Mom to tell me some of her family history. If I had given her a chance to talk about her life, maybe some of her pain would have come out, and I would have had a better understanding of her issues. I did what I thought I was supposed to do, but I wish I could go back and hit the replay button. I didn't know how to ask her to talk to me. Maybe unraveling her story would have helped her. She grew up in a privileged home, but I know so little of her emotional journey. Initiating this type of conversation could be a way of restoring. Helping your mother look at her past could be a way to bring up her painful history and give her a chance to talk about the women in your family lineage. And perhaps it would bring some understanding to your own relationship.

Mom probably did need my validation as a way to show that she mattered, but I didn't know how to give it when I felt so isolated from her. I wasn't quite sure where I had the leeway to share, so often I just retreated. But I'm advocating a different way for you!

You *do* want to communicate on as many levels as possible. It's healthy! It's about the relational investment. It's proactive. It's the opposite of the unwritten rule in dysfunctional families. In counseling circles it's called the "no talk" rule. In other words, in dysfunctional families, there are some unwritten rules, and "no talking" is at the top of the list. The phrase "the elephant in the room" is often used to demonstrate this point. I read the book *An Elephant in the Living Room* by Jill Hastings and Marion Typpo, and I found something I could relate my experience to. The story describes a family trapped in a room with an elephant that represents a family's issues like anger or addiction, but no one speaks of the elephant. Until the elephant is tagged and spoken of, the family remains with the smelly elephant.

Does this sound familiar? A room of people jammed against the walls with a very smelly elephant dominating the space…and no one speaks about the elephant. It's obvious to the reader, though, that the elephant is going to stay in the living room until someone speaks of it, tags it, and removes it. Talking and tagging or addressing issues are huge gifts to relationships if we do them well.

Let's explore some ways to do this. None of us wants an elephant taking up the space that is ours to live in. But so many times we think the easier thing to do is not address it so as not to bring on more discussion and possible hurt. But let's look at how that mentality shrinks not only the room but us!

Ignoring has a place when we are overlooking something we are not called to discuss. This might be someone's own issues they need to take ownership of that you don't have responsibility for. But we are not talking about those kinds of situations. When you know you need to discuss what's between you or respond to your mother or daughter but you don't know what to say, here are two suggestions.

One of the most honest things we can say to our loved one at a time like this is, "**I don't know what to say, but I care about you.**" It's open and humble. One of the greatest mistakes we can make is to launch into advice or "I know what you are going through" sentences that are not very inviting. Many are hurtful and sometimes not needed in the moment. Yes, we've all done that and have seen the injury. Sadly, words carry messages we wish we could take back. We'll cover that in our chapter on forgiveness. But here you want to assure your mother or daughter that you don't have the words but you care about them. It may be all they need to hear in that moment—your genuine care rather than trying to fix, solve, or lessen the blow of what is happening to her by telling her that you have been there too and made it out okay. But that is not what she needs to hear at that moment. She needs to hear that you are focused on her.

Another sentence I have often encouraged mothers and daughters to say is, "**I don't know what to say or do in this difficulty. What do you think we need to do to make things better? What role do you see me playing?**" Do you sense the empty hands and the humility? You can hear the desire for repair alongside the desire for the other's input. Do you imagine the possible brainstorming to follow? Do you feel the beginning of reconciliation?

The initiation of questions is *powerful*! We will discuss this more in chapter 8 on control, but for now, notice how inviting questions are. You don't have to be the one to know what to say—you can invite the other to speak. Where did we get the erroneous idea that we have to have all the answers…and give them to others? It's not fun to be around a know-it-all, is it? But what if the mother or daughter is wise and approachable and open? Whew! That feels so much better and feels like a healthier relationship.

Part of being wise is knowing when to speak. Silence can be golden, but not if we are mute at the wrong time. We don't want to talk too much, but we don't want to seem uncaring by our silence. You have probably seen wonderful dramatizations of people consoling one another without words, and it's beautiful. But at the right time, speak some words, and I am suggesting a very gentle sentence or two for starters. Even if you have been verbally put down or assaulted, you will want to regain your confidence to voice your thoughts by even speaking just a few appropriate sentences.

Especially after a grievous loss or change for a mother or daughter, it's helpful for the other one to say, **"I am so sorry for what you are walking through. I don't know what to say, but I hurt for you/ with you."**

Another really good thing to say when you don't know what to say is, **"How do you see me helping you? What do you need that I can do for you?"**

You may have just winced at that question. Do something for your mom or daughter whom you feel awkward around because of the issues surrounding you, or for someone who perhaps doesn't seem like she even wants you to bring up a conversation with her? Remember, your job is to ask. To initiate conversation. If she can't accept your help, then you have at least asked. You can't force yourself in, but you can offer. It may be the opening thread that helps tie your relationship together at some point down the road that you can't see right now.

There are some other considerations as you are talking with your mother or daughter. You'll want to make sure your words and body language match as you share your heart. Along with speaking words, your body language is saying something as well. Your physical stance and your tone of voice are speaking volumes. Is the message your body is sending the one you want to convey? If you are talking face-to-face, are you using an easy-to-relate-to tone? If you are speaking by phone, do you feel defensiveness rising up in you? Anger or other emotions? It's a good idea to take a deep breath before you speak. Intentionally speak slower than you normally would so you can make sure you aren't saying things too quickly for your mind to register. Words can often spill out of us before we know what we are saying.

Also, have you prayed about the timing of your message? Often, right at the onset of pain, it's hard to hear another person and you can mistakenly turn them away because you are really only thinking of yourself and your situation at the time. You might ask yourself, *Is my mother or daughter ready for me to have this conversation with her? Is it more about me wanting to get it off my chest, or do I sense this would be helpful for her right now?* Make sure your need to talk isn't more important than your mother's or daughter's need to hear it. It needs to be equally helpful and timely for both of you.

I would encourage you also to consider praying and asking God to give you other words if you feel you want to vary from one of these possible scripts with your mother or daughter. These conversation starters are meant to guide but not supersede the inspiration of the Holy Spirit. You will want to also pray for the hearer of your words, and for God to consecrate and bless your time. Your ability to sense how the conversation is going is a big part of talking and inviting yourself into the other's life in that moment. You may come prepared to ask one thing, but have other words prepared so that you don't feel at a loss for words and then resort to frustration or anger. You'll want to pray before and after your conversation so that what you discuss is sealed and affirmed under the covering of the Lord Jesus and so that neither of you can deny His power in your conversation when doubt may want to creep in after your exchanges.

I just finished a conversation with a mother whose married daughter wishes she were pregnant. Asking the daughter questions about her struggle with infertility only produces stress and anxiety for her, as she wishes to have a child. Not saying anything feels very noncaring. So here's a guideline for this scenario for mothers not knowing what to say to an adult daughter in this situation. The words can be adjusted to suit similar situations:

> I care so much about your desire for a child. But I don't want to add stress or even more pressure by continuing to ask questions or by bringing it up. So I am choosing not to ask questions—as much as I want to!—but be assured that I am with you. If you want to talk about it, great. We'll talk. If not, I'm okay with your decision.

Do you hear the respect you are offering, putting the other's need above yours to be close and talk with your daughter? Do you hear your own transparency?

A great skill for families is listening well to one another. Hearing one another and hearing from God helps us reply to our loved ones in a wise and peaceful way. We need to be excellent listeners to words and hearts, and hearing from God for our reply is the greatest gift we can receive and the fruit we cultivate to offer others. God has encouraged us to listen well to others and listen to Him as He leads our hearts to respond.

Some key verses on the importance of listening well to others and how we respond are included below, and more are at the back of the book as a reference for you:

> Be wise in the way you act toward outsiders; make the most of every opportunity. Let your conversation be always full of grace, seasoned with salt, so that you may know how to answer everyone (Colossians 4:5-6 NIV).

> Gracious words are a honeycomb, sweet to the soul and healing to the bones (Proverbs 16:24 NIV).

A good man brings good things out of the good stored up in his heart, and an evil man brings evil things out of the evil stored up in his heart. For the mouth speaks what the heart is full of (Luke 6:45 NIV).

Do not let any unwholesome talk come out of your mouths, but only what is helpful for building others up according to their needs, that it may benefit those who listen (Ephesians 4:29 NIV).

Do not repay evil with evil or insult with insult. On the contrary, repay evil with blessing, because to this you were called so that you may inherit a blessing (1 Peter 3:9 NIV).

Dear children, let us not love with words or speech but with actions and in truth (1 John 3:18 NIV).

My dear brothers and sisters, take note of this: Everyone should be quick to listen, slow to speak and slow to become angry (James 1:19 NIV).

A gentle answer turns away wrath, but a harsh word stirs up anger (Proverbs 15:1 NIV).

And just as there are verses encouraging us to listen well and watch the words we use, there are verses assuring us God longs to speak to us and for us to hear Him. Some of these are below, and others are at the back of the book as well:

The Holy Spirit will teach you in that very hour what you ought to say (Luke 12:12).

Call to Me and I will answer you, and I will tell you

great and mighty things, which you do not know (Jeremiah 33:3).

He who is of God hears the words of God; for this reason you do not hear them, because you are not of God (John 8:47).

Your ears will hear a word behind you, "This is the way, walk in it," whenever you turn to the right or to the left (Isaiah 30:21).

....

Isn't it reassuring that even when we don't know what to say or what to do, God has already provided a way? We come to Him in bold prayers, asking Him to speak through us. And to help us hear His words more than the words coming out from your mother or daughter. God is not a substitute for when we don't know what to do—He is the one who sets *all* of life in motion. He is always ready to give an answer when we ask and help us give an answer to those we love.

Our friend LaTan said she didn't know what to say when her daughter shared her desire to move to another city. She said,

My silence must have come as a surprise to her. It surely came as a surprise to me. Isn't it a momma's obligation to say *something* when her child announces life-altering decisions?

It's an awful feeling when for years we've been the infinite source of wisdom, the one in charge of our children's decisions. Knowing what to say in pretty much every situation life hurled their way. And if we didn't know what to say, we manage to wing it. Leaving the nest is natural. Until our daughter breaks the news she'll be far away.

Whether it was shock or dismay, I stood quietly as my gleeful, green-eyed beauty—my one and only daughter—went on and on. Half listening to her bliss-ful ramblings about how "cool" the city was that she was moving to. As I traced the lines of her beautiful, delicate facial features, her words became distant. Muted.

Time, where did you go? Wasn't it yesterday she was standing on tiptoes, cupping her chubby, little fingers in the air, saying, "Mommy, hold you?" I wanted to hold her. Never let her go.

But I raised her to be strong and independent. To soar, explore, discover new places and new people—wanting her to enjoy all life had to offer. Suddenly the urge to go on—and on and on—came over me. I needed to tell her every single thing. But the crazy thing was, I didn't know *what to say.*

It is possible to be happy *and* sad for our child, all at the same time. For their exuberant joys to clash with our pity-party sadness. But when they are all grown up, I guess that means we should act grown up too.

And so I held my tongue a bit longer. Choked back the temptation to say, "Please don't go!" Partly shocked. Mostly heartbroken. The lump in our throat that blocks our ability to speak. The overwhelming urge to warn them, one more time, against the evils of the world. Encourage them to give more careful thought to this, that, or the other thing. Sometimes our stop button mal-functions. Much like the old Energizer bunny commer-cial, our "something to say" keeps going and going and going—not knowing what to say, yet having much to say and afraid of saying the wrong thing if we do speak. My momma did this—I get it now.

And now that my daughter is a mother, she will get it someday too. Going on and on is every loving mom-ma's loving way of placing a "life's best of everything" memo on her child's soul. How else will they possibly remember all *our* important things? Silently, I hugged her. And maybe I faked happy (a little). Until I truly felt it—later on.

Sometimes as moms we say it best when we say nothing at all but simply love the other when it's needed most.

Mending Thread

It matters what we say and what we don't say. If there's a situation where you haven't known what to say, would you like to write out one of the bolded sentences in this chapter on pages 59 or 60 that you might want to share with your mother or daughter in a letter?

It may not just be your mother or daughter but a sibling or parent who has looked at your relationship or has noticed your difficulty or has asked you about or made comments about it to you. You didn't know how to respond to him or her. But now you do.

How you talk to others about your mother or daughter is also critical. How can you change your language when you aren't sure what to say? Speaking positively even when it's a real choice to do so shows a mature attitude. Sowing the seed in your mind is so important. When someone asks, "How are you and your mother doing?" don't go to negativity. Speak as well of her as you can, even if you don't know exactly what to say. When you don't know what to say, posturing the affirmative of your own heart and how *you* are doing will help bring you to a place where God intends you to be in showing wisdom over your words.

Making It Personal: Saying It with Scripture

Choose a verse from this chapter that struck a chord with you on listening well to others or positioning yourself to listen to God.

How are you going to implement this verse in your relationship with your mother or daughter? Could it look like listening more proactively before you speak? Or asking God how you are to respond before you actually do?

Continue to seek the Lord about how you can implement an honest posture of "I don't know what to say" into your conversations. What are you seeing about how He wants you to recite His scripture when you don't know what to say?

How will you use this to season your speech at just the right time?

You might want to read the verse or verses you have chosen before you start your day and at the end of your day so that they soak into your skin and lay thick on you for any moment you want to speak up and say something to your mother or daughter. This can become a way you discern God's words over your own. Now, that's worth remembering!

4

It's My Part: Responsibly Reacting

Helen

Some of the most healing words a mother or daughter can say to one another are, **"I am sorry. It was my fault. I was wrong. Will you forgive me?"** Using these phrases develops a no-excuses climate. There are always "reasons" for our choices (good or bad), but a climate of excuses doesn't communicate the maturity desired for both mother and daughter. Each time I apologized to Blythe we became closer. I can recall a specific time when I apologized to Blythe for telling her what I thought she needed to do in a particular situation without allowing her to think for herself and make the decision on her own. She was gracious to receive my apology. She could have closed me off or put up a barrier between us for future conversations, so I was thankful she forgave me.

Blythe

I know I put up walls I didn't need to put up when I became a new mom because I didn't want anyone to think I couldn't handle it (even though I had zero experience). I needed Mom to forgive me when I acted as though I was listening to her but really I wanted it to be my idea. She didn't push me, but I needed to ask her forgiveness for my ungrateful heart. As I have gone through my mommy years, she has asked me if it's okay to make a suggestion, and it has freed me from feeling like she's trying to show me I'm not doing something right and to know that it's out of a heart to offer another way to look at or think about something in my mothering.

Helen

I sure want to be known as not trying to own Blythe's decisions or put on myself something that is hers. An overarching general principle for responsibility in relationships is that we're only responsible for our part—we're not responsible for the other person or their response to us. But we are not to incite hurt on the other in the process of defending our words in the relationship.

I remember one day Blythe got off the school bus and came in upset from an experience on the bus. I asked her what happened, but my response to her explanation conveyed that I was sure the bus driver hadn't meant to be unkind. But Blythe felt as though I was taking up for the bus driver and not her. I learned it's really important to take responsibility for your words and allow your daughter to take responsibility for hers, but don't be quick to take responsibility for someone else's.

It's easy to say someone else should have done something, but how often do we look at what we say that's not taking responsibility for our actions? We can mean well, but we aren't owning what really belongs to us. I've learned to take responsibility for my words, not what I meant to say.

We can bet that God's Word has something to say to us about this. The apostle Paul wrote, "If anyone thinks he is important when he really is not, he is only fooling himself. Each person should judge his own actions and not compare himself with others. Then he can be proud for what he himself has done. Each person must be responsible for himself" (Galatians 6:3-6 NCV).

Gulp. Did you catch that last line? "Each person must be responsible for himself." That is a tall order, isn't it?

Do you feel as though even when you take responsibility for your words, your mother or daughter isn't following suit? And it may be hard for you not to judge her or compare yourself with her (ouch!), but that is what this scripture reference is calling us to do. It isn't natural to put that aside and move toward the other person, but if we are going to experience change and see the restoration we so desperately want to see in our relationships, it's worth doing, isn't it?

When you move toward the other person in this way, even if you don't get the response you were hoping for, you are still only responsible for your thoughts and actions. If your mother or daughter doesn't respond, you will have done your part. You can be assured and believe you have done all you could do. And you want to keep the door open for any future opportunities to share again. A response may not come right away. Expect that it might take some time. Know that God has seen your heart and that is what counts the most. It's possible that your words will prompt something to come from your mother or daughter years later. It's always worth speaking up.

This is also when you let go of expectations. They destroy relationships. You can have expectations of yourself but not of the other person. It is natural for us to have expectations of the other person, but we need to learn to let go of them. After all, we do this from the time our children are young. We expect them to talk or walk by a certain age, and expectations follow them into school years. Their teachers (and we) expect them to get to a certain level of proficiency in school, typically marked by grades. But this only goes so far, doesn't it, because soon our children grow up and leave the home, and we can't measure expectations of them by these same standards. In fact, this is the point in life in which we loosen expectations so that we don't have them hanging over our children.

I imagine you may be saying to yourself, *That's the exact opposite of where I am today. If I don't have expectations of my daughter, she won't thrive. She won't succeed. She won't get to the places she needs to go.* But then we have to ask ourselves, "Whose expectations are those? Hers or mine?"

Blythe

I've had experience with this tug-in-your-heart moment. I have expectations for myself but also for my children. I want them to have faithful friends, succeed in school, and shine in the activity they've chosen, which is gymnastics for the girls and Parkour for my son. My older daughter is in her first competition season, and there are things I would love to see happen for her, and yet she has to see them too. She has to want those same expectations, or she will not progress in her gymnastics or in the areas of her life that gymnastics is building, such as courage and patience. I am a "stands sitter," meaning I'm in the stands sitting, cheering her on in her life (and gymnastics!). But I cannot do the work for her or take responsibility for an "off" day.

In the same way, we want to encourage our daughters in life, but we cannot do the work that's required of them nor can they feel we are putting the weight of responsibility on them for our relationship with them. Two people are in the relationship. We need to make sure we are only trying to be responsible for our part and let them work on theirs.

I've been in seasons where I was hoping for things and wanting my mom to succeed in her postchemo journey. But I couldn't make those things happen for her. As hard as it has been at times, I needed to take responsibility for me and not for her. I could share what's on my heart to encourage her, but I physically couldn't do the work Mom needed to do in her rebuilding.

There were times when I was a young adult and she was continuing her degrees and I watched her drive to work, drive to the college or university she attended to complete her classes, and then drive to another state to take care of her parents. She didn't complain, and she took responsibility for what she was doing. I couldn't step in and try to take responsibility for any of that. It was hers, with the help of God, to carry. As I watched her juggle these different tasks, as the daughter it was my role to notice them and encourage her rather than try to take any of the responsibility from her. She was going after it, and it was my job to cheer her on. And she has done the same for me.

During these times, it is like drawing an imaginary boundary line around you and them. As much as you may want to cross over their line, you'll want to stay within the area that is your responsibility. This might be hard if you tend to want to cross over into your daughter's or your mother's space. You can hope for the other person, and you may not even like the choices they make, but it's still theirs to own and not yours to try to influence.

One of the ways this dynamic played out for me was in the area of my weight. During college and after, I saw my weight decrease after I had oral surgery and when I was staying busy in the first semester of college (so much to do for a type A personality!), and then increase beyond what was normal for me. It was my responsibility—I couldn't put it off on Mom for not teaching me how to eat well and keep my weight in check. She would talk with me and ask if we needed to see a doctor about my thyroid and suggest things she thought were helpful. In the end, I had to take responsibility for myself. I couldn't continue to eat the way I had. Exercise had been a part of my life for a long while, but I couldn't rely on that. Something had to change, and I had to let go of the expectations I had of what I would look like and the way I wanted others to perceive me, including my mom. As daughters, we put a lot of pressure on ourselves for how our mother will respond to us and how we like or don't like ourselves, which can then cause us to think our mother couldn't possibly like something about us if we don't. So then we ostracize our moms. It's a vicious cycle.

In this case, I had to put the responsibility back on myself. It did affect my relationship with others and Mom as well. I didn't hold her responsible, but I also didn't want to talk about it much with her. I was embarrassed and felt shame that I had put on myself—others hadn't put it there. We need to remember in our maturing years that when your mother or daughter is struggling, it's a good idea to think about whether it's the time to try to talk about it with them or not. You want to be sensitive to how you bring it up. I didn't fault Mom for trying to initiate conversations with me. But I know I was the one who needed to change my thinking, and that was something only I could do. As mothers, sometimes we want to help our daughters, but sometimes our daughters need to realize things aren't what they seem when it comes to what they think is an easy fix. Sometimes taking responsibility is hard to do.

Expectations of a Mom

Blythe

Not long ago I was talking with a receptionist whom I had gotten to know somewhat over the course of my visits to this office. She shared her excitement of going to see her daughter over the holidays, the first visit in a long time. She told me she is close with her daughter again. She shared that the gap in their relationship was from her daughter's really high expectations of what a mother actually is supposed to be. After this mom's divorce, they had a strained relationship. She said it's taken some time, but now she has a good relationship with her daughter. She said the entire time she kept texting her daughter that she loved her, even though they didn't talk.

This mom knew there were expectations on her that she couldn't meet. And she sensed her daughter had distanced herself because of the demands or expectations placed on her that she couldn't meet. But I love how this mom, my new friend in the waiting room (literally and figuratively), continued to text her daughter and kept telling her that she loved her. And that is a great expectation we can live out: having a mother or daughter communicate to us that they love us, not just in sentences, but also in sacrifices.

Helen

I well remember how I had to humble myself in my relationship with my mom and sometimes with Blythe. You really have to humble yourself before the other. You want to clear out any expectations you have about the other person and put yourself in a position of being the one to take the initiative to "go there" first. And the great gift is that it will be rewarded back to you. Maybe you have expected your relationship to be a certain way and the failure of that poisoned the relationship. It can happen with the mother having expectations of the daughter or vice versa. But it's a silent killer of the relationship.

Looking back, I know my mom had expectations of me, and I could feel it. Daily. Hourly. I would need to look a certain way, perform a certain way, or act a certain way. This led me to be performance based. It meant dressing a certain way and having a certain look in school and participating in certain activities as a child and later as an adult. Her insecurities seemed to manage my life. I felt, "If you perform in these certain ways, you are of value." This can put a heaviness on the other person, and it isn't something easily untangled. Mom's expectations were probably coming from a place of lack or a need. She said things like, "Sit up straight; do this; do that." It was a lot about appearance and grades—performing well.

Sometimes we'll put on the other what we wish we had. This is where good boundaries come into play. I know her behavior toward me could have made me question my own character. But I knew enough not to do that. However, I came to this understanding as a young adult, not as a child. When I received Christ into my life, I heard truth that really changed me. I was in a regular Bible study that I hosted in my home for 12 years, and during those years I heard liberating teachings about not putting expectations on others. Growing up, I thought expectations were normal, but as a young adult I saw my mom still had those expectations. So the teaching I gained became a part of my new understanding of what we are not to put *onto* a relationship but what we are to *own* for ourselves. But I knew then I had been given new life through God's perspective.

A related aspect to expectations is mothers living through their daughters, which is common, but not healthy. Unmet needs in a mother's life is the crash site. Out of that disaster comes a lot of enmeshment, a blurring of each one's unique personality. It can manifest itself in a mother's outside-the-normal range of heavy involvement in her daughter's daily life. Over-the-top yelling and coaching on the sidelines of her daughter's life is a clue. Another signal is an obsessive interest in the details of her daughter's life. An additional place it shows up is in the planning of a daughter's wedding or other life event. A phrase used to describe parents who do this is "helicopter" parenting, or hovering overhead, watching over each part of their child's life.

The message a mom gives to a daughter when she's hovering is that the daughter isn't enough or can't do it on her own. It's a subtle problem in that we are called to be caring parents, but not to live our lives through our children. That's a perversion of the good. If you feel as if you are hovering or smothering your daughter, here's what you might want to say: **"I want to be a healthy mother, but I see signs of living my life through you. I am asking God to help me detach and be a caring and healthier mother. I want you to hear my heart (and words), not to hover over you."**

We don't ever want to take responsibility for someone else's behavior. One of my favorite teachings is from internationally renowned psychiatrist Dr. William Glasser, who is best known as the author of *Reality Therapy* and was a mentor to me. Dr. Glasser's definition of behavior is that "behavior is chosen in order to get a need met. Every behavior is for a reason." In toxic relationships we need to learn to say to ourselves, "Your behavior has nothing to do with me, and I don't need to take responsibility for it." It's helpful to understand why someone chooses a behavior. It's really not personal. You and I didn't cause their behavior. It's not your fault. A mother or daughter doesn't need to own the behavior of the other.

I didn't realize my mom's behavior was not about me until Blythe and Bryan were young adults (in their college years). It was very freeing, and it helped me realize I had not caused Mom's pain. I was liberated, and that continued to help me love Mom through her issues. Because I no longer felt responsible for her and was free, I was able to see her differently. My trying to help didn't work for her, but at least I didn't feel responsible. I could have been angry with her, but I had more compassion for her. She had social anxiety and didn't feel like she fit in. Yet she placed herself in those social settings and then used me as a scapegoat for all the frustrations she was having. I had thought something was deeply wrong with me because of all the anger she had toward me. Mom acted out of her need to feel at peace and right with herself and her surroundings. It didn't have anything to do with me, but it sure felt like it.

We act for a specific need. So how could we be responsible for another person's behavior? When our children say, "You made me mad," we remind them, "I didn't cause you to get mad. You felt the emotion of anger and then you acted on it. But I'm not responsible for the way you behaved."

Is that a huge relief to let go of thoughts that it was about you or because of you that your mom or daughter acted the way she did? We can remove all the pressure from ourselves when we realize we are not responsible for our mom's or our daughter's actions. The guilt and shame that can come with taking responsibility for things that are not ours can be overwhelming. But you can release those emotions; you don't need to carry them one second longer! Was there a big *thud* as this burden fell to the floor?!

What's Behind Our Behaviors?

It's helpful in our relationship with mothers and daughters to understand some of the underlying needs behind our behaviors. What is it that drives you to believe something about yourself or your mother or daughter? Often it begins as a thought that drives you to act upon it, and before you know it, the thought becomes real to you and you feel that you must tackle it head-on. But our heads don't always give us the accurate picture. You know in your heart what's true of your mother or daughter. But your head convinces you to think and act in another way. It can be a cycle that's hard to break, can't it? How do we get an accurate picture that doesn't lead us to do things in a rash moment or out of desperation but that's filled with truth and sound beliefs? How do we realign our thinking so that we aren't instantly acting out the way we always have?

Looking at your needs and taking care of yourself without trying to take care of the other person is a start. You don't need to feel guilty for their actions and choices. You care about them, but you aren't carrying the weight of their choices or the responsibility of them.

Our friend and a beautiful writer Bekah says it this way: "You can care without carrying the weight of another. There are areas I carry in order to keep life moving along hunky-dory. I carry the belief that I have to be a good friend. Be a fun mom. Have positive insight to share at every given moment because if I don't, perhaps my faith is faltering. Why do I carry so much? What happens if I put down all the people and responsibilities I'm carrying?"

She is a passionate soul who has walked through many different relational shifts, moving and releasing old and new friendships, and she only has her mother now that she lost her dear father several years back. She shares, "I released myself of the unnecessary weight I carry in order to keep the status quo comfortable. Have you listened deeply to your own heart's confessions? What would happen if you stopped giving, carrying, fixing, helping, advice-giving? How would you feel? Heavier? Lighter? Release all those protective layers. Underneath is love."

Underneath is love. When it gets down to it, as Bekah says, it's about the love underneath all of the messages that have built the layers of our carrying what others have put on us. She so rightly asks, "What happens if I put down all the people and responsibilities I'm carrying?"

Picture in your mind how you have been carrying your mother or daughter around on your back and your life is weighted down. Imagine taking her off your back and letting her find her feet and caring for her without carrying her. It's a lot to think about, isn't it? For years we've done life the way we could manage. And the idea of taking off the responsibility of others leaves us thinking, *Well, now what do I do?*

I think the key is knowing and resting in the fact that God created her and God can hold her up—you don't have to. He knows whom He put you in relationship with because He designed you for each other. He knew she should be *your* daughter. You should be *her* mother. It wasn't a harsh punishment or a mistake. He knew how you would bring glory to Him through your relationship. Your ability to show love to her after she shared words that cut through you. The goodness of God in your heart not to cut her off when it would seem the thing to do. We know there are times you physically need to distance yourself from an overbearing loved one—even a mother or daughter. But most often we will be called to minister to someone in the area of their greatest pain and our greatest need: to be known and loved and seen for who we are.

We see this playing out with mothers and daughters. It is super healthy to help shape each other in a positive way. What we just described is a fluid relationship between mothers and daughters that should be a normal part of the relationship and influencing one another for good. Damaging messages and behaviors can influence negatively. They can slow down or halt the process of how you respond to each other's input in your lives. But when there's openness, there's a gift of receiving from the other that can go well beyond what you think you will benefit from.

Blythe

My daughters have helped shape me when I've been open to their input and not resistant. We were on a particular shopping trip, and we found a kitchen store and needed to replace some items in our kitchen. I thought I knew what we needed, but while we were walking around the store, Maris figured out what we should get, and my belief I knew it all was debunked! She was right and played a big part in getting what we needed. It helped me see that she has helpful suggestions and knows more than I think she does. I don't always know it all or have it all down pat. I learned to listen to her more. I needed to show an openness to receive the gift of insight she had that went beyond what I thought she could contribute.

Likewise, Calyn has helped me see that she knows how to take care of herself when I am open to letting her explore rather than dictating to her. She is showing me that she picks up on things I'm not aware of. At eight, she blends up a great smoothie for herself and gets herself what she needs to eat without my always doing it for her. We have a tendency to think our children always need us to *do* for them. But they don't always need us to do; however, they do need for us to *be* there for them. We are gaining less of a *doing* status and more of a *being* role in their lives as they get older. They are shaping us by showing us they are ready and capable of being more independent, and I can't hold on to the little girls I still think they are. I need to be careful in how I talk with my girls and how my words shape them as much as my actions.

At all times we need to guard what we are thinking and what we say to our mother or daughter. This verse speaks to us so specifically:

> The good man out of the good treasure of his heart brings
> forth what is good; and the evil man out of the evil

treasure brings forth what is evil; for his mouth speaks from that which fills his heart (Luke 6:45).

We are to look at what's in our heart because the "mouth speaks from that which fills his [or her] heart." It's hard to argue with sound advice, isn't it? Especially from the One who created both you and your mother or daughter. But exactly how do you look at what you are responsible for and let go of all that she is responsible for but isn't taking on herself? Let's go there, shall we?

Steps to Un-Take the Responsibility of the Other

We believe there are steps to undo the ways we have tried to take on the responsibility of the other. This is a hard undoing, because mothers and daughters have a specific relationship that is unlike that of a mother and a son or a father and a son. Perhaps it is related to the fact that mothers often see themselves in the face and ways of their daughter. Maybe it started when the daughter was young, or maybe it came about during the years when their adult lives overlapped. The mother sees who she has become through her daughter. The daughter sees what she doesn't want to become.

Some daughters have had to bear the weight of responsibility for their mother's choices. Some mothers are living out of the choices their daughter made that have landed them in an early grandmothering role. No matter how we got to the point we are in our relationship with the other, there is a way to release the "grabbing on" of how you have acted toward the other if you have taken on too much responsibility or have expected too much of the other.

First, you want to own your part.

One of the hardest sentences to say is, "It was my fault." But it's a mark of maturity. It helps bring restoration and mending. Our default conversations seem to make excuses for our behaviors. But owning them is a part of healing our heart and our relationship with the other person. Have you noticed that when you first say, "I misunderstood," "It was my fault," or "I made a mistake," how often the other person comes closer to you more quickly? And how it frees them to admit their part? They may not always admit theirs, but you have created what we call a warm environment for them to do so. It was as though you invited them into your home, and instead of a cold atmosphere, you prepared your heart and your home to receive them by diffusing any awkwardness or strong feelings. This is a really healthy way to approach relationships, and you will be a leader for doing so. James 4:10 states, "Humble yourselves in the presence of the Lord, and He will exalt you." When you humble yourself, you are essentially saying to God, "I recognize Your presence over my own, and I choose to receive what You have for me."

Second, ask God to show you some of your responsibilities in the relationship.

It's a good idea not to presume what your role is, but to ask God to give you creativity in how you approach your responsibilities. Ask God first before going to your mother or daughter. Here are some examples:

- Are you a grandmother who is trying to offer too much discipline to your grandchildren and it's frustrating your daughter? Get creative in your approach with a signal between you on how you can discipline without overstepping your daughter's preferences or style.

- Are you a daughter who belittles your mother in front of her and others because you are trying to "help" her? You feel she's lost touch with how she needs to act or what she needs to say and you are trying to edit her. How much of this is necessary? How can you speak to address your concerns but also honor her (even if you don't feel she deserves it)?

- Are you a mother who doesn't put any limits on what you

allow your grandchildren to eat and do when they're visiting you? And it makes it hard on your daughter when she takes them back to her house? Should your role be more aligned with how she prefers things?

- Are you a daughter who thinks your mom should not come over unless she's invited? You want your role to be more of a manager of the relationship, but her free spirit rubs against your style.

You can start by saying, "**I see that we have different ways of approaching our relationship and my grandchildren/my children, and I'd like to make sure that we are thinking along the same lines in our relationship.**" You can state what you see currently and what you'd like to see happen. It's such a help for everyone to see where things are and where at least one of you wants them to go. It's hard for things to ever "get there" if you never speak about the problems. You may even want to list out issues and go over them so that you're both checking them off in your mind as you talk.

Also, you may need to say, "I recognize that I have talked down to you when we're together and I see that it's *my* challenge to speak more favorably of you. I am going to own my thoughts and not put them on you. You may continue to say things I don't agree with, but I am no longer going to say words that pull you down."

Third, get an idea of whether you are to be serving more or serving less or planning more or planning less in the relationship.

If you are more of a word picture girl, you might want to attach a word picture to what you see as your role and ask if your mother or daughter agrees with that. For instance, your word picture might be more of a school administrator type and your mom is the social coordinator at the school. It's all well and good until the social coordinator organizes something that interrupts the school administrator's well-thought-out calendar. It might be that your word picture is COO of your home, but your mom is a founder in the family. The founder needs to trust the COO to do her job and not interfere but take responsibility when she isn't giving the other what she needs to equip her and speak words that inspire, not impede progress. Founders often carry a vision, but at some point they need to trust the COO to carry it through. Another word picture is the designer and the decorator. One of you is more driven to visuals of what things should look like (the designer). The other is the decorator and makes use of what you have. If one of you is visual and one is more "it doesn't matter what it looks like," you'll want to talk about how these two worlds can mesh as it applies to how you operate in your relationship.

You can come up with your own word picture and talk about what you see and then ask the other to share who she is in the scenario. Having a fictional "person" to identify with might take some of the pressure off labeling each other.

One of you may be more of a carefree spirit and the other is purely structured and strict. The two of you have clashed over things such as when to have holiday gatherings and who is responsible for what, or when the grandchildren can visit. Being as honest as you can helps accelerate you gaining a closer victory with each other. It might help to have a printed calendar that the two of you can look at together and plan out what you are comfortable with before the calendar gets too full and thus creates more stress between you.

As the mother, you might ask your daughter questions like, "**How would you need me to serve you in these upcoming weeks when you start your new job?**" or "**How do you see me being a person who serves you rather than stresses you?**" You'll want to talk about how many times feels comfortable for you all to plan something together. Her idea might be twice a month when yours is twice a week. So obviously you need to establish a meeting ground. But the idea is to dig into how much you serve her and how much you plan with her.

Conversely, as a daughter, you may say to your mother, "**Do you know how I see you sharing in my life now? It's not by how much time I see you but by the quality of our visits. If you can help me with _____ when you come, it will free me to be more present in our time together.**" Or, "**I really appreciate it when you do _____ but not when you do or say _____.**"

The mother-daughter dance is a tough one at times. A doctor who is a family friend told us of an experience he had witnessed between his mom and his sister. One wanted to instigate one action and the other wanted another, thinking it was best. He shared: "Young moms crave knowledge because they lack experience. Both moms and daughters want to do the right thing, but defining what the right thing is can be a problem. Knowledge and experience—it's hard to compromise and hard to convince that one way is wrong or insufficient. It can be a difficult dance."

Experience and knowledge go a long way in your relationship. One is gained over time and one is hopefully passed on to the other. We encourage you not just to think that exchange is a top-down from mother to daughter but it can also be daughter to mother. Keeping the highway open between you is what we want to advocate for you so that you build bridges rather than roadblocks.

Fourth, recognize the season you are in and settle your heart within it.

The responsibilities for mothers and daughters change with the seasons of their lives. God is the one who can help us update our approach depending on the season we are in. It doesn't mean you settle for less than you are or where you are. But for the season, it's where you stick. And this season can be an investment of intercession. Interceding for your mother or daughter is when you pray for God to speak to them just as you pray for Him to speak to you. Praying scripture over them is a great thing to do, especially when you don't know what to pray. Start finding verses that mean something to you and resonate with her situation. You can do a word search on verses that speak to God's faithfulness. And you can repeat the words of the scripture like it's a prayer over your mother or daughter. This is one of our favorite things to do as we find scriptures that speak to our hearts.

Helen

There are numerous scriptures I prayed for Blythe as she was launching into her career and dating. I wrote her name and the date in my Bible next to some verses such as Psalm 9:9-10; Psalm 20:1-5; Psalm 40:1-5; Isaiah 58:10-12; Isaiah 61:1-4; Psalm 16:6-8,11; Psalm 17:8; Psalm 42:8; Isaiah 30:20-21; and Isaiah 41:10, to name a few. The one I have marked a lot for Blythe's future spouse started 11 years prior to Blythe's wedding date and is Psalm 20:4-5: "May He grant you your heart's desire and fulfill all your counsel! We will sing for joy over your victory, and in the name of our God we will set up our banners. May the Lord fulfill all your petitions."

Blythe

Seeing my name in Mom's worn, heavily used Bible next to verses and knowing where and when she prayed for me is a treasure I don't take for granted. After Mom was diagnosed with lymphoma and as she underwent chemo treatments, I texted and emailed Mom prayers to remind both of us who our God is and how we could trust Him and turn to Him even in difficult days. Some of these were 1 John 4:18; Isaiah 58:8; Psalm 20:6-8; Psalm 9:10; Psalm 28:7; Psalm 91:1-2; Isaiah 26:3-4; Romans 15:3; Isaiah 53:5; Hebrews 4:14-16; and Jeremiah 17:7-8. For periods of days I would type these verses as I read them and send them to Mom so she could easily see them while she was in chemo or on the days after when she didn't feel well. In particular, there was one thing I shared with Mom about Psalm 57:7-8,11:

> My heart , O God, is steadfast, my heart is steadfast; I will sing and make music. Awake, my soul! Awake, harp and lyre! I will awaken the dawn…Be exalted, O God, above the heavens; let your glory be over all the earth (NIV).

I emailed her:

> I picture God getting glory from both of us in whatever kind of trials we are experiencing. We bring Him pleasure just by being who we are—God's glory is over all the earth even through us. I'm praying for God to fill you in every way so that you feel your body rising up to the healing already expressed in it and your continuing to stand and fight against all hindrances that are not God's design for your body and that you have the power to overcome through Christ. Even though the symptoms appear, you are not bound by them nor defined by them and they are not signs of weakness but God's power to complete His healing of your body.

Sometimes sending prayers to your mother or daughter can allow you to express your heart to God for what you know to be true or are desiring to see in this season, and those prayers speak to the other person in a way that directly spoken words can't. Sometimes the words of those who experienced a close relationship with Jesus in the Bible can penetrate our hearts in ways that show us that we too can have that closeness with Him. And He can heal hearts, especially those of our mother or daughter, and bring life back into the relationship. Often we've found that asking God to give us words for the day really have the power to bring us out of a place of despair or discouragement and into a place of His provision for us.

When you use these four steps we have just outlined in this chapter to "un-take" the responsibility of your mother or daughter, we believe you will experience freedom in your relationship. And it also positions you to be able to more freely love her when you have put back onto her what is hers to carry. It is a healthy step to take—not one born out of a mean spirit or a prideful attitude. It is one of surrender and a choice to, in this season, break off what has tethered you together. It's time for her to run her course, and for you to run yours.

Mending Thread

What do you think is the main reason your mother or daughter doesn't take responsibility for herself?

What if instead of spending time thinking about what has happened in the past, you use your time to think of how things can be different in the future?

Spend some moments thinking about what you would like to see between you. Resolve to take care of only what you are responsible for, even if she does not take responsibility for her part. What is a standard phrase you can say if you start to see her not taking responsibility for herself? And what is your cue to remind yourself when you are veering into her territory? You might want to ask her to say her phrase to you and vice versa if you start noticing the other going into the other's lane.

How do you think only handling what is yours will change your relationship with your mother or daughter?

> The LORD is my strength and my shield;
>   my heart trusts in him, and he helps me.
> My heart leaps for joy,
>   and with my song I praise him (Psalm 28:7 NIV).

This is assurance that the Lord will help you. You have someone going before you, and you aren't just winging it. Can you handle your heart leaping for joy because of the praise you offer to God? We often do this when things are going well in life. But when we can do this even when we are frustrated, hurting, or unsure of our days, we show Him our trust is in Him and not in our efforts. Know that God honors a humble, fixed heart that wants to please Him more than even those He has put in our lives. Let's live this out!

Making It Personal: Write Your Job Description

How often do you get to write the job description you want to have? Well, now's your chance! What if you were to write what you are responsible for—only you? Not what your mother or daughter is responsible for, but what you are responsible for. If it would help you to write what you are *not* responsible for, you can do that as well.

You may want to share your job description with your mother or daughter as an act of obedience of what you are only responsible for. What will *not* be included and what you want to make sure you're clear on is what is in the lane of your mother or daughter. Okay, and go!

Be sure you put your description somewhere you can see it and reference it (for example, maybe place it near the phone because you feel a sense to call your mother or daughter more regularly than you need to). Progress will come when you can not only use this when you are prone to take responsibility that's not yours but when you begin to internalize it and you no longer need to think about what's yours and what's hers.

5

Forgiveness Finder: Aiming for God and Each Other over Offense

Blythe

There's a game we used to play as kids. Maybe you played it as well. Four brightly colored game pieces and color-coordinated cards and spaces rounded the game board. The object of the game was to send someone home if you landed on their space. Oh, how I dreaded the word *sorry*. The game is one I have played with my children, and how often I want to avoid the "sorry" mandate when the roll of the dice calls for it!

In the real sense of saying "sorry," my mother showed my brother and me how to quickly address anything between us. Our tendency was to just say, "Sorry," but Mom gave us as young kids a more thorough example of how to address forgiveness. In the previous chapter we talked about how to move toward the other person. In this chapter we want to go deeper and address how you seek forgiveness and grant it.

Helen

As someone who loves the word *restoration*, this is the part I love to share! My children even know me so well that when we are watching a movie, they say, "Mom would like this; it has restoration in it." It's true! As a counselor and a student of the Bible over the years, I recognized that there are three kinds of forgiveness:

- From God

- From a person you have offended

- To another person when you have felt offended

In this chapter we will share verses about these three distinctives of forgiveness and give you specific language you can use to experience all three kinds of forgiveness. We will also look at what we can do when we get it wrong (which is hard to swallow but it does happen) and give you words to repair damage. We want to equip you for every conversation you have.

The first level of forgiveness we experience is when we become believers and ask God's forgiveness for the things we've done—past, present, and future. We thank Him for His forgiveness and recognize that we need it. We believe in the One who can grant forgiveness that no other god or religious spirit could touch. And it's this primary need to find forgiveness in God that enables us to go on to the next steps. Without it, we don't have the capability or the heart to forgive others or ask for forgiveness ourselves.

The second kind of forgiveness is when we have offended someone and take the steps to clear our offense by a three-step process. This is what I taught Blythe and her brother when they were children. Even children can follow this because of how practical it is. It doesn't need to be a long, drawn-out process. But clearly and simply articulating these words will be so helpful.

- "I was wrong. I am sorry. Will you forgive me?"

Or

- "I have offended you by _____ (lack of love, my bitterness, and the like). I am sorry. Will you forgive me?"

Asking the person you have wronged this final question brings closure even if they say no, they won't forgive you. You've asked the question, and that completes it for you regardless of their reasons. Sometimes we don't get the forgiveness we ask for, and it's hard to understand why someone would want to hold on to their anger or resentment for months, years, or even a lifetime. We have all heard stories about those who hold on to unforgiveness, and we can see the negative spiral their life takes. I've known people who have harbored unforgiveness in their hearts for years, and sometimes they are very sick and are still unwilling to forgive. I've seen people in their last days extend forgiveness, and I have witnessed what an impact it's had on a family member.

We don't want to wait until we're in a desperate situation to extend forgiveness. Not only does forgiveness restore the relationship between you, but it points to the forgiveness we have experienced with God. And it's another way to follow God and practice obedience by giving the forgiveness He has extended to us.

Unforgiveness is toxic for both you and those around you, in addition to the one(s) you aren't forgiving. The poison goes deep and wide and impacts future generations if you don't take care of it in your heart. In the very difficult times with my mother, I remember knowing I needed to forgive her—whether she ever asked my forgiveness or not.

I can think of other numerous situations in which some mothers and daughters have refused to forgive, therefore resisting the grace that comes when we forgive someone who may or may not deserve it. They won't let go for various reasons. One reason is that the toxins fuel their fire, and if they let go, it will be necessary to live without their scapegoat. Many people want to blame someone else for all the things that are wrong in their life. Not to forgive another is a lot about power and control as well. Unforgiveness is a huge red flag in our mental, social, and emotional health. It's unhealthy and damaging to those around us, but especially to our own hearts. A healthy stream of water becomes toxic when toxic materials run through it. So we encourage you to process any unforgiveness and ask the Lord to bring light and understanding for what is beneath it—and the courage to choose to set someone free.

The third area of forgiveness is the most subtle and difficult: when we are the victim. This is when we need to forgive someone who has hurt and offended us. They may never even apologize or make amends. They may be deceased or in jail or another place you can't reach them or oblivious to their offense. But we remain their prisoner until we let the offense go. There are so many women with "mother wounds" because of the unfinished work of forgiveness.

The good news here is that even if your mother or daughter has wounded you and they never ask your forgiveness, you can be set free. You can forgive them. You don't have control over them or their choices, but you do have control over what you do. Your ability to forgive your mother or daughter determines how you experience life, walking around free rather than with an enslaved mentality. There will be a lightness to your walk when you aren't carrying around the weight of your thoughts about her and why she won't initiate asking forgiveness.

We have to remember that sometimes people become blind to their own faults. If they have hurt you and probably others, they may have blinders on when it comes to their actions. You could tell them (and maybe you have) all day long that they have hurt you. But there is something in their spirit that isn't hearing you or accepting their participation in hurting you, and that will not change no matter how many times you bring it up. There is a spirit in their heart that is rejecting any responsibility for hurting you. However, you aren't stuck there. They may be, but you aren't.

Then there are some who are oblivious to hurting you because they have done it for so long that it's no different from getting up and getting ready for work that day. It's part of their life. So you will want to point out to them in a time when you have a settled spirit and in a kind and loving way something along these lines: **"Mom, I know you may**

not recognize how you hurt me with your words, but it does hurt. I choose to let them fall away, and I don't hold on to them in my life. I forgive you." Your choosing to forgive her is not contingent upon her asking you for forgiveness. You don't have to receive the words "Will you forgive me?" in order to issue them yourself, and this is what is powerful about this exercise.

Or you can say, "As your mother, you know I love you and want you to be happy and to have the very best in your life. But there have been times that your willingness to say or do whatever it takes to get there has hurt me. When you said _____ or when you left the house without explanation, it hurt me deeply. You aren't responsible for my emotions, but I've held back from you the hurt I've felt, and what I want for you is to have good relationships in your life and that nothing is missing in ours. I forgive you and ask you to forgive me for any hurt I've caused you."

You can take these suggestions and make them fit your unique circumstance and use different words, but this gives you an idea of how to initiate conversation and how to take ownership of your thoughts and words and not put them on the other person.

Helen

My mom never made amends or asked for forgiveness. It was difficult not to ever hear those words. She was an avid Alcoholics Anonymous (AA) attender and then leader. Steps 4 through 9 in AA are about taking responsibility for your family, asking forgiveness, and owning your disease. The 12 steps, which you have probably heard, are: We

1. admitted we were powerless over alcohol [our addiction]—that our lives had become unmanageable.
2. came to believe that a Power greater than ourselves could restore us to sanity.
3. made a decision to turn our will and our lives over to the care of God as we understood Him.

4. made a searching and fearless moral inventory of ourselves.

5. admitted to God, to ourselves, and to another human being the exact nature of our wrongs.

6. were entirely ready to have God remove all these defects of character.

7. humbly asked Him to remove our shortcomings.

8. made a list of all persons we had harmed, and became willing to make amends to them all.

9. made direct amends to such people wherever possible, except when to do so would injure them or others.

10. continued to take a personal inventory and when we were wrong promptly admitted it.

11. sought through prayer and meditation to improve our conscious contact with God as we understood Him, praying only for knowledge of His will for us and the power to carry that out.

12. having had a spiritual awakening as the result of these steps, we tried to carry this message to alcoholics [addicts] and to practice these principles in all our affairs.[1]

She taught the 12-step program, but she never asked me for forgiveness. However, there was a time in my life when I told her I chose to forgive her. The freedom that came when I did that was gratifying, even though I really wanted to hear her initiate that conversation and ask my forgiveness. But that never happened, and I knew I needed to bring it up if it was going to be addressed. I believe she wanted to make amends but perhaps felt like she had done too much damage. Perhaps she just thought I had already forgiven her without words.

There are many verses in Scripture calling for these three kinds of forgiveness. But the rarely discussed verses are the ones dealing with this third area—our forgiving those who have hurt us and who haven't owned it yet, and might not ever own it. Counseling offices are filled with these tender stories. I have walked with moms and daughters who couldn't face the other to say these words. I recommended what each could do. Most of the time I think they needed validation that there was hurt, but I have wanted mothers and daughters to see that no matter who initiated the hurt, both have a reason to walk through forgiveness together. In the end, it isn't about who did what, but how you reconcile.

Here are some of the verses that encourage us—the victims—to seize forgiveness. They are clear and compelling. There may be a couple you want to take and make your own and insert your name where it says the word *you*. Personalizing scripture helps us see how God's Word comes alive and is meant just for us. Its authority has power over your life.

> Bless those who curse you, pray for those who mistreat you (Luke 6:28 NIV).

> Forgive us our sins, for we ourselves also forgive everyone who is indebted to us. And lead us not into temptation (Luke 11:4 NIV).

> Peter came and said to Him, "Lord, how often shall my brother sin against me and I forgive him? Up to seven times?" Jesus said to him, "I do not say to you, up to seven times, but up to seventy times seven" (Matthew 18:21-22).

> Whenever you stand praying, forgive, if you have anything against anyone, so that your Father who is in heaven will also forgive you your transgressions (Mark 11:25).

> Let all bitterness and wrath and anger and clamor and slander be put away from you, along with all malice.

> Be kind to one another, tender-hearted, forgiving each other, just as God in Christ also has forgiven you (Ephesians 4:31-32).

> Bearing with one another, and forgiving each other, whoever has a complaint against anyone; just as the Lord forgave you, so also should you (Colossians 3:13).

In case any of us wonders how important forgiveness is, these verses talk consistently about how Christ has forgiven us. And they emphasize that we should also forgive those who have wronged us. We see this as an act of releasing your mother or daughter (or any other person in your life) from any idea that you hold power over them in forgiving them or not. It's acknowledging and choosing forgiveness so that you are not gripped by not forgiving someone. We don't want to become indebted to someone else because we won't release them.

I love the following quote by Lewis Smedes that speaks to this idea of unloosing the gravity between you and experiencing the heart lift that comes when you do so. He wrote, "When you release the wrongdoer from the wrong, you cut a malignant tumor out of your inner life. You set a prisoner free, but you discover that the real prisoner was yourself."[2]

Put another way: "We must forgive others so we can have relationships. Anything you can't forgive begins to master you." These are words well-spoken by my pastor, Mark Cowart.[3]

Words Marking Forgiveness

We want to live free, so what do we say to the one who has hurt us? I would ask God what you need to say, but here is a short and simple example of what it might sound like, either spoken or written: **"Because God has forgiven me, I forgive you."**

If you have mother or daughter wounds and she is deceased, you will still need to forgive her. We believe saying those words out loud is the best way to address this. You are still tied to her, and even though she is not present anymore, you want to wash your heart clean and purify your mind through the words you are declaring to forgive her. This is a powerful way to let go of the tether to her so that you are no longer carrying an unhealthy and unholy attachment to unforgiveness.

Similarly, you may also want to write a letter to repeat these words to reflect the desire of your heart to forgive. You should truly experience a measure of freedom and healing as a result of releasing her. You are not tied to her any longer, and you are cutting ties with anything that was remaining in her spirit around you and in you. This is where breaking off generational ties is so important, which we'll talk about in chapter 9. But for now, know that when you take this step to free yourself of someone in your family—mother or daughter or others— you will be setting up freedom for those in the next generation. What a beautiful gift you are not only giving to yourself but also to your family!

If you have a mother or daughter wound and she is living, sharing these things with her in person would be of great benefit to you both. Speaking face-to-face creates a strong connection, and it's why Jesus was seen so fully by those who were around Him. He looked people in the eye and told them they were forgiven. And can you imagine how free they felt to see that in His eyes?

If you don't feel you can meet in person, you can write these words of forgiveness in a letter and send it. This will also be a powerful gesture from you to her. When written, your words won't be misquoted and can hopefully reach a place in her heart where you might not have direct access.

If it is either emotionally unsafe or physically unsafe to connect in person or by written word, you can reach freedom when you speak these words out loud to yourself. Your words have meaning and purpose behind them. God hears them, most importantly, and you have taken some ground in asserting your forgiveness that no one can take

away from you—not even our enemy, Satan. And when you forgive
or have been forgiven, you know how your heart soars because of it.
When freedom is granted, no one can accuse you of remaining a prisoner. Satan would like you to think so, but you know the truth.

We get an example of forgiveness in Matthew 18:21-35 where Jesus
told the story of a king who extended mercy and forgave the debt of
one of his servants. But his servant misappropriated that mercy and
went out and found a fellow slave and began to choke him, demanding
he pay back what he owed. The fellow servant asked him to be patient
while he worked to get the money, but the servant who had had his
debt canceled had him thrown in prison. Others saw what happened
and told the master, who then reminded the slave that he had been forgiven and asked him if he should not have mercy on his fellow slaves.
Jesus then went on to say that each of us should forgive our brother
"from [our] heart" (verse 35). We must decide to line up our hearts with
God's heart and extend the mercy we have been shown by God.

Our good friend Stephanie feels she took this wisdom to heart after
she lost her mother and didn't have the opportunity to ask her forgiveness. She shared,

> Looking at the outside of my body, you could find a
> multitude of physical scars. Most of them from surgeries,
> some from carelessness. But the inward scars are count-
> less. Many of these are deep and dark. Recently I heard
> about Kintsugi. It's the art of precious scars. When a
> ceramic piece like a bowl or teapot breaks, this Japanese
> art uses liquid gold, silver, or other fine metals to bind
> together the broken pieces, creating a unique piece that
> can be displayed with pride. This is me. God had to break
> me completely so His light could shine through me, just
> like the gold in Japanese pottery.
>
> My adolescent years would fall into the childhood
> adversity category. My bowl had been chipping away

from my earliest memories. But when my mother lost the fight with ovarian cancer, I was shattered. It was too late for me to say I was sorry for the countless acts of selfishness, disobedience, and worst of all, insensitivity. After all, I was 19 and had all the answers.

In hindsight I can see how much help my mom really needed. At the time, I felt as though it shouldn't be my responsibility to care for my younger siblings or tend to the house, and I had to miss out on Friday night football games or aimless activities with friends. I didn't really know how to process my emotions in a healthy way and would burst into a screaming match with Mom just before she would leave for the night shift at the hospital. Note her work. She wasn't leaving me with this burden so she could go out for a ladies' night or party; she was trying to keep our rundown roof over our heads. As an adult now, I know how hard it is to keep a household running and feel the anguish that comes with leaving my family behind for business trips. Through the years of prayer and scripture, God has worked on dissipating my memories of anger and replacing them with memories filled with compassion for Mom and me.

Growing up, I craved having her home. Not just so I could come and go as I pleased, but so that we could just be together. The crazy thing is, I prefer to be at home with my family on Friday nights now rather than being out on the town. My craving to be at home and for Mom to be with me is still just as strong now as it was then. Especially when I fail at parenting. When I am not as grace-filled as I should be, usually when I am overstressed and running on fumes, I get a better understanding of what my mother faced every day. She had four children pushing her buttons, and she was working full time at night so she could make more money, but never having enough sleep or money to make ends meet, and in her last years of life she did it while on chemo. I wish I could have been more gracious to her.

I never understood why those years were so tough and why God took my mother from me so early in life. I was angry and distant from God until I felt there was nothing left of me. This is when I met Him at the cross with my guard down. I said I was sorry, and the mending began. When I broke into pieces, it was generational curses of brokenness and poverty breaking too. When He bonded together each broken piece, I was being redesigned to do things differently. I needed to be a different kind of mother, wife, friend, and sibling than the generations before me. I needed to be aware of women's health issues and how our bodies handle stress. Most importantly, I had to learn to forgive.

The Magnitude Effect of Forgiveness

Helen

Have you ever noticed how people focus on the magnitude of an earthquake? Neither Blythe nor I live in areas of the country where earthquakes are felt, but we do hear about what others have experienced. The magnitude determines the extent of damage. And, in a similar fashion, the magnitude that you forgive others determines the degree of healing that occurs. Will that be a lot or a little? What does forgiveness do? It clears the air. It diffuses built-up anger. It builds a bridge between you.

The example you set with your mom or daughter is also something you'll want to do with your children or grandchildren as well. It creates an atmosphere for healthy family discussions and carries over into other relationships. The mother-daughter relationship is a primary relationship since it's a relationship of origin. When you start adding a spouse or children, you are expanding forgiveness to equally important but secondary relationships—those that came after your relationship of origin. The relationships you didn't choose—the one between you and your mom—and the relationships you have chosen—your spouse or the father of your children are all part of this.

The relationships in your life need the covering (much like outer layers) of forgiveness over each one, and you are the person to bring this to your family. Outer layers of plants and skin often protect, don't they? Forgiveness acts as a barrier, a seal over your family. When forgiveness is in place, there aren't any areas left open for anyone to bring up what's in the past. It's a protection from further hurt and an inner knowing that you have covered this ground between you.

"Both healing and hurt come through relationship," says Pastor Cowart. "You have an unprecedented opportunity to go to the next level—forgive the person who was wrong and keep your heart pure, then be wise."[4] This is the heartbeat of moving forward. And this is where we have the ability to go to the next level through forgiveness and move forward in wholeness together.

Another way to think of it is wellness. Wellness means the absence of sickness. And a well-put-together relationship is one that is full of health. You have the opportunity to introduce wellness into your family where maybe it hasn't been felt or seen before. You are an instrument of healing in this family. Forgiveness isn't just an act we walk through; it's a way of life we choose. To keep accounts between us clean and open. To mend a tear where it has ripped your family. To mend what appears to have shredded the communication between you.

You are the first step in making this healing happen, and you are more capable than you might imagine. You have more influence than you probably give yourself. When you initiate forgiveness, not only will it free you, but it shows you have qualities of a leader that are respectable and desirable. You are helping the other person see that being vulnerable together is far better than being vulnerable alone. We want your forgiveness to be a marker where you can both think, *Remember the day we both settled it* (your forgiveness with each other), and you can go back to that day as many times as you need to. Forgiveness often isn't a one-time thing—we hurt each other, and it's not usually just once. So repeating the steps we listed here will continue to be a lifeline between you.

A dear friend, Jennifer, shared about what happened with just four simple words: "Will you forgive me?" She told us,

> Something happened so long ago that I can't pinpoint what sparked old memories to rise to the surface. All I remember is that it was connected to a deep-rooted insecurity that started in my childhood with me believing that I wasn't smart or good enough. I had no idea this painful insecurity would resurface in my thirties, but I'm glad that it did because it caused me to seek further.
>
> I was too young, I suppose, yet discerning and sensitive enough as a young girl, to understand what broken looked like. I understood how brokenness happened in the heart of my mother and that most of the time for her it was fear-based desperation, driving her not to turn out like the ones who led to her brokenness.
>
> She wanted me to be different from my father and excel in life and school especially. But learning for me involved learning how to shut down when I heard yelling, and eventually Mom hired tutors because her trying to teach me basic mathematics was miserable. However, I have many wonderful memories too. These cords and strands of my life came from so many people in my life: my mother, my pastor, my mentors, and my best friends. They are a part of me—they helped to shape me.
>
> My journey is woven tightly in my faith, grounded deeply in moments of prayer, and a feisty determination that comes from my mom, who encouraged me to be better. If I'm honest, she pushed me pretty hard, but I have her to thank for lighting a fire inside of me to rise above

the statistics stacked against broken girls and products of divorce.

> Two are better than one because they have a good return for their labor. For if either of them falls, the one will lift up his companion. But woe to the one who falls when there is not another to lift him up. Furthermore, if two lie down together they keep warm, but how can one be warm alone? And if one can overpower him who is alone, two can resist him. A cord of three strands is not quickly torn apart (Ecclesiastes 4:9-12).

One day she asked me four simple, yet powerful words: "Will you forgive me?"

We cried and hugged in the shoe department, and then she bought me the most adorable shoes. She needed to say it and feel my acceptance of it. She needed to free herself and explain her reasons behind pushing me so hard. She was the driving force in my life who just wanted to make sure I had the best life. She wanted to make me wake up from what she called my "dream world." But my la-la land seemed a lot nicer at times, and every now and then I still visit there, my head in the clouds and my heart willing to forgive freely as I have been forgiven. Motherhood is not easy, and the mother-daughter relationships can be the most powerful and painful ones, but surrendered at the feet of Jesus, you can be certain that God can redeem hard moments and memories and cause relationships not only to heal but to flourish.

Mending Thread

There's a story in the Bible about a woman who poured perfume on the feet of Jesus and wiped His feet with her tears. A Pharisee, the naysayer in the bunch, remarked to Jesus that if He were a prophet, He would know who was touching Him and what kind of woman she was. Jesus shared with him the parable of the two who owed money to a moneylender who canceled their debt and He asked the Pharisee, "Which of them would love him more?" (Luke 7:41 NIV). Simon said the one who had the bigger debt canceled. Jesus reminded him how the woman had put oil on His head, poured perfume on His feet, and kissed His feet, and then Jesus said this: "Therefore, I tell you, her many sins have been forgiven—as her great love has shown. But whoever has been forgiven little loves little" (verse 47 NIV).

How big is your debt toward the other person? Do you see yourself forgiven because you have loved much? To the degree you are aware of how much you have been forgiven, you will have the capacity to love more. In this story, the ability to receive forgiveness isn't based on how good you are or what you've done right (or not right). It's on how you love. You recognize that you have gratitude toward the mother or daughter you love and you aren't going to let unforgiveness stand in the way of your relationship.

Making It Personal: Focus Forward

After forgiveness is offered and received, don't look back at the past. We spend far too much time focusing on what is behind us. First John 1:9 shows if we confess our sins He will forgive us. It's done. After you do this, put up a "No Fishing" sign. Don't go back there and fish for it again.

Would you consider making a sign that flags this forgiveness in your life? What would it say? Do you have a board of wood you can paint on (or buy inexpensively from someone who sells wood) and create a visual reminder of the fact that you have a new heading? This is what rules over your mind, not the past. You could even craft something out of distressed wood or buy one that is already done for you. Craft fairs are great places to meet those who do this in your area and could make you a custom sign. Or if you have anyone you know who is a crafter or woodworker, why don't you consider this as a gift to yourself for Mother's Day or have a close friend help you with it? This can be placed over the mantle of your home or office, and it can also be a mantle over your heart, a visual of the words that frame your life.

A wise idea would be to focus forward. Why spend time on what you've walked through? What is the image you see when you see you and your mother, or you and your daughter in the present and in the future?

God doesn't want us beating up ourselves or others after the forgiveness conversation. It's done and it's behind you. Now you want to look ahead at what's between you in this new place. Do you recall how God delights in doing new things? God dealt with Israel in the days when they were not calling God "God" and were worshiping other idols and making themselves and their lusts a priority. There were people who suffered greatly for not acknowledging God as the one to worship and bow down to. But when He saved His remnant in Israel, they recognized God was starting a new season, and His power was seen and felt as recorded by Isaiah.

God has been doing something new in each of our lives when we bow to Him and not to our own ideas of what our greatest needs are. As you come to Him and seek what He's doing to tear down what's been in your heart, even toward your mother or daughter, what do you see when you look up from there?

6

Words That Can Bring You Back Together

Blythe

I've said several things to my children I wish I could take back. Trying to teach lessons when they're on the way out the door to school. Or trying to give advice about the next day right before going to bed. Right? Not right. On one particular occasion, I remember telling my daughter Maris what I had been noticing about her attitude. But it was crushing to her. And I remember not wording it well. And my words sent her off in tears. On one busy morning, everyone was rushing to get to school on time, and I chose precisely the wrong moment and tone to speak to Maris. It wasn't a good send-off, and I knew it the minute the words exited my mouth.

Why did I think having these "quick" words before school or at bedtime would bring restoration? I hadn't properly set things up to be the right environment to talk about the things I needed to guide my daughter on. And of course, these conversations didn't lead to restoration, only resentment. So on the morning of the send-off, I drove to school and found her during lunch and asked her forgiveness and told her how much I loved her. I couldn't stand the way it made me feel to know I (my words) had caused her pain instead of safety. Criticism instead of loving correction. She embraced me and thankfully wanted me at the lunch table with her. Whew!

I want to seek to restore the relationship between me and my daughters because I don't want anything to stand in the way of our communication and their feeling love from me. They get plenty of opportunities at school to feel let down by others, and I don't want to give them even one opportunity to feel that between us. They may not know the words of repair yet in a specific or relational sense, but it's never too early to start modeling it.

Why is it that words have such power? Have you said things you wish you could roll back onto your tongue and into your mouth and have a do-over? The backspace key is one of our favorites, and yet it's only reserved for typing, not talking. No wonder we are a texting world when we can self-edit before our words spill forth!

Helen

Here we are again at my favorite word: *restoration*! I suppose it's because I've needed it so very much in my life, and I long to see people invite restoration into theirs. Blythe has told me I am the "word coach"—she loves writing words, and I love speaking them!

When it comes to words, every one of them matters. Some words will be a blessing, and some will be a judgment or a curse. The subtle message attached to or behind your words also conveys a blessing, judgment, or a curse. Listening and speaking to your mother or daughter— or others about her—affects your relationship. Your words can also create a ministry of reconciliation between the two of you. We'll share words that invite reconciliation and words that do not.

Some of the words we have chosen not to say to one another are "you never," "you always," "if only," and "you should." These are blanketed statements that place shame on the other person and convey the message they didn't get it right. And these words don't promote reconciliation—they tear down the other person. They have the ability to make that person feel they are always messing up, when the truth is that probably some of the time they are doing things well. But you don't want to use one thing between you to represent all things.

The following model is one we do not encourage because it does *not* invite oneness. In the counseling world, many therapists teach clients a conversational skill set for expressing one's personal needs in hopes of coming closer in a kind of reconciliation with the other party. The script being taught is: "When you do _____, I feel _____, and I need [you to] _____." Think about it. It's a healthy thing to be able to speak up for your needs, and it's healthy to exhort one another when it's appropriate and done well. But do you hear the dependency? With these words you are basically communicating that if the other party would just meet your needs and stop doing such and such, there wouldn't be a problem. The first two parts are okay, but not the third. We can't change the other person or make her do something.

We really need to take that truth to heart. No matter how hard or how long we try, we can't persuade or expect another person to change. There's a better way—let's talk about it!

There are two other scripts I have used and taught others to use that have been more successful in bringing about reconciliation.

I have encouraged them to say, **"I want us to have a good (healthy, great) relationship. We do have a problem, but I believe we can make repairs. What do you think we need to do to make things better?"**

These words are simple. They are putting the goal of reconciliation out there first, admitting there's a problem, and inviting the other party into the resolution. You are not the know-it-all. You are asking for the other person's feedback. The script is inviting and not hostile. Usually small children using a simple version of this script come to a resolution in minutes. Adults may take a little longer because they are often dealing with deeper issues. But these sentences are short enough to remember and easily accessible for you to share with your mother or daughter.

This is a great starter and doesn't do any harm to either of you. You are starting the conversation and then after inviting the other person to give her feedback you have the freedom to share your ideas as well.

If it is more comfortable for you as either the mother or the daughter to write this in a letter or email as opposed to saying these sentences in person or sharing them by telephone, that works too. Sometimes it's even preferable to write it out so your words are not twisted and your emotions don't overtake the conversation. It takes courage to speak. But your heart is wishing for repair, and this dialogue creates an equal playing level for both of you. One of you isn't holding an imaginary measuring stick over the other's head about what she has done, causing her never to measure up.

A similar script I use came out of a terrible mistake. Years ago as a school counselor, I rushed through a parent-teacher conference out of time pressure and went straight to my concerns about the student. I could see such disappointment and pain on the mother's face. She needed to hear her son's successes first. Ouch. I learned not to skip that step again. That night as I agonized over my mistake, the Lord gave me "The Sandwich."

Here is what I should have said in a conversational sandwich to the student's mother: "Your son is doing an outstanding job in these ways in the classroom (top soft bun). I do have a concern to share with you (tough meat in the middle), but I believe we can work together to help your son be even more successful (bottom soft bun). May I share my concerns?"

This is how the "sandwich" might sound for a mother-daughter conversation: **"I long for a great relationship with you (top bun). Even though we have/share some real concerns (hard middle), I believe we can begin some repairs and make things better (bottom bun)."** Then add, **"What do you think we need to do to make things better?"**

This is similar to the previous one, but you can see subtle changes in presenting the elements you might wish to say. It adds a layer that's often really necessary between mothers and daughters, which is recognizing you don't want to be in an awkward relationship and you want to work on whatever you can to have a better relationship.

A valuable takeaway is that *we need to say something positive before we share our concerns. Moreover, it's important to ask permission to share our concerns!* We'll talk about this more in the next chapter.

But what if your mother or daughter doesn't respond when you ask how you both can make things better? If there is silence, don't lose heart. Sometimes these things can take some time. If it becomes clear that she doesn't know what to say or isn't sure how to respond, you could offer, "**I can understand if you want some time to think about it. How about we talk again in _____ (a week, Tuesday night before I pick up the kids, and the like)?**" This way you allow her some time to process, but you are putting a specific time frame on it rather than just saying "later on."

Reconciliation is a dance. The relationship of a mother and daughter is an even more delicate dance. Women catch every nuance about a sentence: the tone of voice, the timing of a response, any harshness, any control, any (false) pride. We are even super observers of the unsaid. The dance of the unspoken things is obvious for those who read body language!

Didn't your heart soar when Belle in *Beauty and the Beast* began to dance in the grand ballroom? The dance was a reconciliation as were the lyrics to the song. If you listen to the words of the song "Tale as Old as Time," you'll see what we see that's so fascinating. It refers to learning new steps, leaning into each other. And when one was willing to yield to the other, even in a slight way, it led to a deeper acceptance and a softening, an opening into the other's heart.

That's us! As mother and daughter, one of us usually bends to the other—even small expressions can have an effect, and the one who is leading, as in a dance, helps move you toward unity or a place of coming together. Even just a few words that aren't full of emotion have the power to open the door for change.

The idea of seeing that we could be wrong, and in fact were wrong, is a tough one for us. We don't like to be wrong, and we work not to be. However, sometimes we need to be aware we aren't always seeing everything. We miss things sometimes, and we are not going to get it right with our mother or daughter unless we are willing to acknowledge our part in the fracture of the relationship. Sometimes we need to learn some things that humble us. Our mother or daughter sometimes doesn't see things like we do. And often it requires us asking God, "Help me see where I am missing my mom. We just aren't on the same page," or "God, show me where I am not seeing what I need to see with my daughter."

Blythe

At the first of the new year in 2018, I was believing God for a lot of things. I was believing Him for my mom's further healing and restoration to life. I was reminded that I loved her so much, and to the degree I loved her, it hurt me to see her suffer.

I know others are in a season of battle with their family, even their mother or daughter. I know you may even be in a physical battle of the wills between you, and you think it's impossible for mothers and daughters to be close. But with Jesus, it is possible. With Him nothing is able to keep you from forgiving and loving each other.

An article from *Charisma* by author and speaker Cindy Jacobs that I read in the early part of 2018 said this: "Satan will say to you, 'You're never going to have a good relationship with your family. You're not going to have good times. The things that have happened have caused irreparable damage.' No, that is not true, because it's not God's will, and God created your family. He meant it to be good. Don't give up your battle. Now, maybe it won't come about in 2018, but don't give up the battle. God will turn it."[1]

"God created your family. He meant it to be good. Don't give up your battle" are strong statements that I believe have the ability to help focus our feet forward to keep moving despite what we feel inside. God created you both, and He knows there isn't the closeness between you now, but it's worth pursuing. Don't give up—it's worth it to work toward the completion of your family relationships and the way God designed families to function.

We can't let words keep us from the type of relationship God wants us to have. As much as it is up to you, don't let anything stand between words spoken over you, actions taken against you, and beliefs that have settled in you. You are deserving of a restoration that is far above what you expect or what your mother or daughter expects. Will you be the one who takes steps to grant this to the other?

Mending Thread

Blythe

Reconciliation packs a lot of punch in such a big word! Reconciling has the tone of each coming closer to the other, doesn't it? Yielding to each other, not holding back, but inching your way closer to your mother or daughter. One of my mom's favorite phrases is "patch, patch." We often say this when we are mending something, but it's also what those who sew do. They patch and sew, and sew and patch. It's an act that brings something new to something old. And isn't that what reconciliation is? Bringing a new definition between you on top of what's been part of the old.

What can you do to sew into your reconciliation? What words are coming to mind? If you ask God to supply it, He will. He knows what's between you and the words that have done damage between you. Will you allow Him to bring words of reconciliation that are needed for today?

We can have assurance that when we ask God for something, He will answer. A key passage that affirms this is Luke 11:9-13:

So I say to you: Ask and it will be given to you; seek and

you will find; knock and the door will be opened to you. For everyone who asks receives; the one who seeks finds; and to the one who knocks, the door will be opened.

Which of you fathers, if your son asks for a fish, will give him a snake instead? Or if he asks for an egg, will give him a scorpion? If you then, though you are evil, know how to give good gifts to your children, how much more will your Father in heaven give the Holy Spirit to those who ask him! (NIV).

As a good Father, He gives you the Holy Spirit to help you discern where you are to venture with your mother or daughter in the words you exchange to bring reconciliation between you. How will you start to receive this gift from God?

Making It Personal: Forgiveness Cards

Earlier in the chapter, we shared words you can use with your mother or daughter when you are seeking to make things better between you. Ultimately these words will help bring about forgiveness. Write out the words you can share with your mom or daughter in versions you feel you need to use for your unique situation. These can be printed on cards that you pull out for reference or tape on your desk where you make calls or they can be digital images.

What will you say to your mother or daughter? How do you feel like you relate to her right now? It will be important for her to hear what you see in the relationship.

How do you see yourself with your mother or daughter? Does she seem unwilling to talk and do you know why? Ask if she is willing to share what needs to happen for her to talk with you again. Often when people (this is especially true with the mother-daughter bond) know how much you miss them or want to have a relationship that doesn't cause hurt for either of you, they will tend to listen when you humble yourself by initiating forgiveness, even if they haven't asked for it. It's a powerful motivator to draw you closer together.

As you do this, ask others to pray for you. When you have an army behind you, it makes the journey with your mother or daughter one you can sustain, with support, and also allows them to see answered prayer and join you in the restoration of your relationship. It increases your faith and belief that change and a lasting relationship between you is something that is not just for all the other daughters or mothers, but is for you! You have the ability and the tools you need to be reconciled to your loved one, but that first step is yours.

7

With No Permission Comes No Advice

Blythe

I remember coming home from the hospital in our big SUV with our first child, Maris. Mom and Dad were following behind. Maris was wedged in her car seat with one of those head rests that looked like it would overtake her. Mom and Dad were with us when Maris was born, and I can remember Mom asking, prior to going to the hospital, if we needed to have the fire department look at how we (she and I) installed the car seat in the car because neither of us wanted to read the manual! Instructions from others are often hard to follow because it takes time and investment. And it can feel invasive into our personal abilities.

Do you like reading instructions? When someone who really knows what they're talking about is telling you how to work something or how to do something, do you listen? Mom and I are not fans of instructions. We put them aside and ask our husbands or another person in our family (usually a man!) to read them. It just isn't pleasant reading. And it takes us away from the time of using the thing we bought.

And so it is with advice giving and receiving, isn't it? It's not pleasant when we aren't expecting it or don't want it. If you have a daughter, you know the eye-rolling you get when you start in on something with her. If you are the daughter, you know how you feel when you hear "I think you should_____" or "You need to _____," or other sentences that sound like your mom has just the right thought for you or instructions for you that she sees would make your situation better. It takes away from our relationship and our joy with each other.

Once I started sharing what I thought would help one of my daughters who is in elementary school. The response was, "But, Mom, you don't understand." And I thought, *She's probably right.* I wasn't at school; I wasn't attending her classes each day and sitting with her friends in the lunchroom. I was displaced from her situation, yet I actually tried to put myself in her place. I didn't ask permission—I just started in. Later I had to ask her to help me put myself in her place and see the situation from her perspective. She needed to give me instructions on how to approach this so I could understand her circumstances better. Without permission, no advice. That's the focus of this chapter.

So how do we stay away from advice giving and how do we ask to give feedback with permission? We desire a good relationship, but sometimes our efforts in building it go awry. Let's look at how to avoid the advice-giving trap.

Helen

I grew up with a mom who consistently gave me her advice on a lot of things. Having someone do that to you can make you feel like you aren't capable of making your own decisions and that you must have "missed it" somewhere. I think some people generally think their job or way to help others is to offer advice to people. Often it comes from their need to feel good (or better) about themselves.

Unsolicited advice, especially from a mother to a daughter, is not only unwelcomed, it feels punitive and invasive. Asking permission before giving advice, ideas, or feedback is the key to a relationship that doesn't feel like the other is too involved in your life. You are asking if it's okay to share, and your posture is one that conveys more of a suggestion that they can accept or toss out. You can preface it by saying, **"If this feels right and you want to keep it, then great, but if it doesn't feel right, then let it go."**

Blythe

I can remember Mom asking my permission to give feedback when I was a young adult on my own in the great big world in front of me. I remember feeling as though I had a choice in receiving her ideas or feedback. It gave me a sense of control and ownership over my life, but with the oversight that she could provide wisdom as someone who had been in the places I hadn't.

When it came to how I should handle situations in college dorm life or how to handle disappointments that came, I knew Mom had a knack for asking if it was okay for her to speak.

And she continued to do this as I made decisions after college about where to live, whom to have in my life, how to focus my job interests, and other areas. As I ventured more and more into my own territory, I knew I had the freedom of an available listener in Mom, but not an overbearing advice giver. She asked permission, so I felt I could listen to her suggestion or advice and decide if I wanted to incorporate it in my decisions. And I think that is one of the biggest gifts we can give our daughters—asking questions as a mom to clarify needs that sometimes daughters figure out on their own just by the other asking questions. And less of "Let me tell you what you should do." That feels like an automatic cue for a shutdown.

Years later, when I told my parents I had met the man I wanted to marry, I remember their response: "Well, if God has confirmed this for you, who are we to say anything different?" I remember thinking that was the most freeing statement I could have heard. The translation to me was, "If God has shown you, then we trust you." And after only two months of knowing this man, God was showing me he was the one my parents and I had prayed for all of my life. They didn't try to offer advice or give feedback. Their trust in God for me superseded any need to ask questions or say anything that would have seemed like questioning.

As I've parented my children, Mom has asked from time to time, **"May I make a suggestion? What do you think about saying this?"** or **"Is it okay if I share some feedback with you?"** or **"Is it okay for me to give you an idea of how to help that situation?"** And it paves the way for me to say yes or "No, not right now." Most of the time I have taken her advice because it really was good feedback! Sometimes I have filtered it through what I was thinking about at the time and taken bits and pieces and applied it with mine.

There was a time when this didn't go well, and we have acknowledged it and healing has come in our relationship as a result. When my children were small and Mom felt concerned I was doing more than my share of taking care of them and that my husband wasn't noticing some of the ways he could help me, she wrote down her thoughts and sent them to us both. To us it didn't have the same tone of "May I share?" but was more concern and feedback we didn't expect. And it did put some space in our relationship with her. My husband and I talked about it, and we knew Mom cared deeply for us and wanted the best for us, but we felt the timing and approach maybe weren't the best, and we didn't know how to respond at first. Maybe you have been in a similar situation and can relate. What did you do in a time like that?

We did what we thought was best—we talked about it and shared it in a counseling session. It's hard when you are not in regular communication with your mother or daughter because you sense you need to "leave and cleave" to your spouse out of respect to the command in Genesis 2:24: "Therefore a man shall leave his father and his mother and hold fast to his wife, and they shall become one flesh" (ESV). I knew I wanted to honor my mother but also honor the one God had given to me to direct and help lead my life at that point.

So that's what I did during that time—I held fast to my husband and listened to his thoughts, and we talked about how we should respond. We did it together. We believed talking about it in a healthy way would give us the response we needed to share with Mom.

My husband and I took the necessary time to process our thoughts together, and when we reached out to Mom again after a short period of time of not being in contact, the healing began. We knew Mom loved us and her heart for us was good. Talking about it brought us closer again. There was redemption for all of us because we talked about our relationships and how we were functioning as a family and how we could support each other.

And since then, if there has been a time we have felt that she has shared something in a way that didn't meet with our spirits, we have been able to say, "I'm not sure about that, but we'll consider it" or "I'll think about it." We have been more receptive because of growing in our relationships together, and there has not been a time since then when Mom has shared something we didn't want to receive feedback on.

As family, sometimes we instantly share our response, while other times it might take some time to process it. This is something that's key. When you have a situation where the other is giving you feedback and you either don't agree, you don't think it's accurate, or you think it's accurate but you aren't sure of the delivery or how you're supposed to respond, you might need to come back to the conversation if you can't address it right then.

You might not be able to give an absolute yes or no to them asking if they can share some feedback. And you may need to say before they share, **"Because I can only address one situation thoughtfully at a time, please share your comments on only one thing now and not anything else, and we can look at anything else after we've worked through this one area."**

Sometimes as a mother we want, and maybe need, to pour out all our heart to our daughter. And timing and approach will be key for you as you do this. Sometimes as a daughter we need to put some time between us and our mother so that we can sort out what is being communicated and how we're going to respond. As the mom you may even say, **"Right now I just need to share this with you, and it's more of my processing than it is directed to you. Are you okay with my just sharing and getting this from my head to my heart while we talk?"** This may help you get to the core need you have to share as you process and give your daughter an understanding of how you are arriving at the conclusion in a safe, protected conversation. But you want to be careful you don't overprocess or start blaming but give bullet points to get to what you need to share.

When there is a good relationship, the results can be good. If there is uneasiness between you on any level, then any type of advice giving will not be received well. You *always* want to clear up anything between you relationally before sharing what you want to share with the other.

This might look like:

- "I don't feel I am able to hear what you want to share until we are clear on what we are working toward in our relationship."

- "I have felt offended when you have shared _____ with me in the past. Can you affirm to me that you want this conversation to come from a place of love in your heart and I will commit to do the same?"

- "Do you have expectations that what you are sharing will be implemented or is it more of a chance for you to share how you are feeling? I want to understand if you are sharing because you want to transition it from your mind to me, or if you believe it's something I need to hear." (In other words, you are asking if their need to share is greater than your need to hear it.)

- "Can we put aside the major decision we need to make

together and first talk about the last time we spoke and where things left off? I believe that will help us as we move forward."

Once you establish these and any other questions that are appropriate to ask, you are ready for the change in your thinking from advice giving to offering a suggestion. It may not seem that different to you, but it's all in how you present it and in your expectation of the response from your mother or daughter. Changing your approach in speaking with your mother or daughter often is a change in the perspective from which you share.

Change in Perspective

Blythe

There's a line that I really like from *Willy Wonka & the Chocolate Factory*. If you aren't familiar with this story, a wealthy candy factory owner has five golden tickets placed inside candy bars that are shipped all over the world. Five lucky winners get the chance to tour the factory and receive a lifetime supply of chocolate. Charlie Bucket and his family live in an impoverished area with not much more than the clothes they have on. Charlie finds a coin that gives him the chance to buy a candy bar, and he becomes one of the winners who tours the factory. After the other four children show their true colors during the factory tour and after Mr. Wonka tells Charlie that he won, they lift through the glass ceiling of the factory in a glass capsule. Mr. Wonka asks Charlie if he liked the chocolate factory, to which Charlie says, "I think it's the most wonderful place in the world."[1] Wonka proceeds to tell him that he's giving it to him. And as Wonka shares why he wants to give it away, he says, "Who can I trust...? Not a grown up. A grown up would want to do everything his own way, not mine...I had to find a child. A very honest, loving child."[2]

Here's the thing that speaks to me. Often as grown-ups, we do things the same way time and time again. Children see a different approach; they bring in a new perspective, and that's what we want to do in our sharing with each other as mother and daughter. Charlie gets to bring a new perspective to running the chocolate factory. He doesn't have to do things the way Willie Wonka did. He gets to decide how to run the factory using his own ideas and from his perspective. He doesn't have to follow someone who has done the same thing day after day and year after year, and he doesn't have to get unwanted advice.

And isn't that the dream for us? We get to determine, together, how as mothers and daughters we want to live in our relationship, not from a place of hearing unwanted advice, but with a chance to explode through the glass ceiling of the constraints we put on the other. Permission encourages relating; advice is isolating.

Helen

Most people don't like to be told what to do. Children often don't like to be told they need to do anything. And adults are the same way, whether you are the daughter or the mom. There's a way to ask your daughter if you can give feedback when you see it. There's a way to tell your mom what you think of how she's doing things. What you don't want is escalating conversations or outbursts that don't get you closer to each other. If you've hit that point, then try to bring the conversation into focus by going back to the conversation or source of frustration. Have the conversation again and explain what you want is to share, not shove. Share your heart, but do not shove it on the other person.

When mothers and daughters aren't doing very well, often one may feel like the advice the other person gave or the way it was received wasn't what they expected. Then they typically move apart from each other rather than come toward each other. It seems unnatural to walk back into what just drove you apart.

But here's how you do this in a healthy, productive way: "**May I share some thoughts?**" or "**May I share a concern?**" or "**Are you okay** with my giving some input?" Wait for a response. If they say no, don't proceed. Honor their boundary. At a later time, they may ask for you to share your feedback. But again, the relationship is more important than your making suggestions.

Your other relationships might be healthy and solid, but you just can't understand why you and your mom or daughter aren't doing well. It could be that your mom didn't approve of your choice of whom to marry or where to start your family. It could be that your daughter doesn't approve of you getting remarried or how you spend more time with her sibling's family than hers.

It could be the relationship has been strained, and you feel like you should give advice or feedback to "help." But what your daughter really needs is for you to ask if it's okay for you to share. And then be willing to pull back if she says no. Or, if she says it's okay to share but she doesn't like what you suggested, be willing to put the relationship ahead of trying to be seen as a good advice giver. Remember, most people don't like to be told what to do. They want and need to figure things out for themselves. Think of yourself as a good conversation starter and don't always try to get something from the other side. A good percentage of the time, we want to offer conversation, but it may not be reciprocated. But we can try to engage them in a genuine way, and this could be another step toward building bridges with the one you love.

How do you do this? One way to do this is to say, **"Would you like to talk about _____? Is there any part of you that would like to know what it was like for me when you were the age of your youngest? Do you want to know how I handled things like that with you?"**

Or if you are the daughter and you want to initiate asking your mother for advice, make sure you give proper boundaries for what you are asking for. **"Mom, in this moment I'm asking for your help with _____. I may not need it past this one instance, but right now I'm asking for you to tell me what you think."**

When you give feedback, the implication can be the other person didn't think of it on her own so it can feel like you have all the answers. You want to be careful in what words you use so that you aren't causing the other to feel as though she messed up or could mess up if you don't share. You want her to believe you have something to offer and that it's adding value to her life, not taking it away. If you can remember that unwelcome advice is not a help to a relationship, then it will change how you speak to the other and how you feel about her. Instead of seeing yourself as someone who gives advice (maybe you do this with others too), you can become free to enjoy what's there and not feel as though you have to fix it or improve upon it. You can pray that God would help you not be the one trying to fill in the gaps but that He would show you what you can do that would be edifying to the relationship.

It may be you have a mentor for the things you feel you didn't get from your mother. Someone who has guided you or affirmed you as a daughter. But you still want to look at how to restore your relationship with your mom if there has been a breach in your family and in your lives. Breaches are meant to be repaired. Even if she is not a mother you would say you look to for teaching and wisdom, it is still possible to have a relationship with her that's not based on what you can learn from her to further your own mothering skills. You can look at how you can relate to her in the place you are in now as God leads you to acknowledge the role she has played in your life and the role she can play in the future.

So what does mothering look like if you do not have a good example to follow? While you are still working on repairing the relationship with your mother, you could think you don't want to mother like your mom did. She gave too much advice; she didn't approve of you. She always told you rather than asked what you thought. Maybe it's your daughter who has turned off the communication with you because you gave too much advice. How do you approach her? How do you gain her trust so that she doesn't associate you asking her questions as trying to give feedback on her life?

Blythe

When Mom asks me if she can give me feedback, I feel the freedom to say yes or no. I'm not forced to say yes. There were times where I would have felt like, *You don't trust me or think I'm making good decisions so you're telling me what you think.* But I began to see her asking to share as a noninvasive way for her to offer a suggestion without it feeling like advice. Permission to talk is so much better than giving advice, which automatically puts you on the defensive. As a daughter, you have an opportunity to think it's out of a heart to see you prosper and not out of your mom's need to project on your life what she wishes she could have had with hers. That could be part of it, but hopefully you can recognize if that is happening and let it filter out of your conversation.

How do you trust what she is going to share? Give her the benefit of the doubt. Don't automatically assume it's going to be a negative or irrelevant point in your life. Having an open mind is the key to any relationship, and this is perhaps more important in the mother-daughter relationship than any others. Two women—usually women are very strong in their opinions—looking at life from two different life seasons. She may not have earned your trust up to this point, but don't discount it for present and future conversations.

I look back now on what I would have missed out on if I had not listened to Mom's suggestion about something that has been a very needed addition in my life: Zumba. She was enjoying going to a class in her area, and she knew I loved dance. When she suggested it, I told her no, I didn't think so. I just couldn't think about what it would look like. I didn't want to veer from my normal routine. I didn't think her suggestion could enhance my life the way it now has. But I tried it with her and I loved it! And it is one of my most favorite things to do now. If

I had not listened to her suggestion, I would have missed out on one of the things that gives me great exercise and enjoyment, but even more than that, I would have missed the goodness that comes from listening to suggestions and not automatically thinking, *It's not for me.* We can do that when our mother offers something and we tune it out. But why don't we give it a chance? We can't automatically think what our mother is going to offer is not going to be good for us. In fact, it might just be the thing both of us need to do together.

And for us, it represents far more than just Zumba. Mom would go to Zumba as she was trying to reverse the symptoms of Parkinson's, which she was also dealing with, and it was a way she kept moving and pushed ahead in the healing of her body. And so when I was doing Zumba while Mom was going through her comeback journey post-chemo, it was a reminder to me of the goodness of listening to Mom, and exercising when she couldn't, which brought me closer to her in my heart. And Zumba was keeping me healthy during the time I was caring for her.

I don't think either of us have verbalized this, but I see how something Mom loved became something I loved, and I probably wouldn't have pursued it if I hadn't seen what it meant to Mom. And it became something that brought us closer together, and that's another angle that has helped in our relationship: having things we like to talk about when we do talk about harder things. The point is we had to fight for what brought us enjoyment and seek safety in our suggestions. Those things didn't just find us.

As we grow and mature as daughters, we might not have listened to our mothers when we were in our teen years or even after. I know I didn't always. I thought I knew better. As I have become a mom, I see how much I really didn't know when I was younger. And I understand how hard it is to be a mom with so many decisions and responses to give to your children. It makes me appreciate my mom even more. Now I want to hear her feedback because I realize I have so much to learn. If I can learn from her, maybe I won't make so many mistakes as a daughter and mom.

I realize there are many daughters who have been wounded tremendously by opening their heart to a mother spewing her words without thinking how they would come across. And I have done the same thing to my daughters. I have seen characteristics in them that I have criticized and I have hurt their hearts. Instead of asking if I could tell them what I saw, I just went on and spilled it out. And most of the time I have come back to them asking for forgiveness for how I handled my words and hurt their hearts.

As they become teens, I want them to feel as though they can come to me with anything and that I can ask them for permission to speak into their lives. If at all possible, it needs to start early. The patterns I build now with my daughters will affect our relationship in the future, and I want to build good bridges of communication with them.

Mending Thread

Think about developing a cue for yourself when you feel the need or desire to control. Give yourself time to make sure your response isn't advice. You might want to think about putting some time between what you heard and how you are going to answer.

Some examples would be pausing or waiting even longer to speak than you would normally, or changing your physical stance or sitting down so you don't seem as defensive. Developing some cues will help you remember what you need to look out for so that you can think before you speak. If control has been an issue, you may want to wait hours or days before you offer feedback or respond to your mother or daughter.

How is it that words come so quickly but actions take years to cultivate? We don't want to expect that our words will immediately change the shape of our relationship, but they can. We believe words have the power of life or death. And we believe speaking life is part of taming the tongue. Is your tongue a weapon of defeat or a tool to bring power and strength?

Making It Personal: Asking Permission with Childlike Wonder

Think about when your kids ask you permission to be with friends, eat chocolate before dinner, and the like. Think about how much you appreciate that (when it happens!). You are in a position to say no, and you appreciate being asked. My kids ask me if they can use the iPad, have a certain snack, or buy something with their own money. They are so hoping I will say yes and they are risking asking. Let's piggyback off these requests from our children into asking permission to speak to our mother or daughter about something rather than assuming she won't give it to us or doesn't want to hear from us. Sometimes children will say, "I know you probably won't let me do this, but..." or "I know you probably don't want me to have this, but.." They go into it with a negative attitude, but they are still wondering if it's possible. Do we do that as adults?

When we ask permission to speak into our mother's or daughter's life, we can't automatically assume it's a yes or no. But it can be a lead-in to a bigger conversation. Your child respects your authority (at least some of the time, hopefully!). In the same way, you want to respect your mother or daughter, whom you are trying not to control but get a response from. Maybe it has been about control in the past, but now you see this isn't what your daughter or mother wants from you. It might meet your needs, but it doesn't meet hers.

As a mom, instead of thinking about how much you could help your daughter, think about *what* you can provide to her and how you can meet a need in her life that she recognizes, not just one you recognize. You don't want to control her decisions but find ways to add value to your conversations without sounding as though you're trying to give advice.

Most of the time our children are after what meets their needs in the moment. How can we be like that and ask our mother or daughter what they need or want without it sounding like we are trying to step in with our ideas? Further, how can we not let it be about what we will gain in giving feedback but how it will benefit the other person? Our thought process should not be how it will help us to share but how this could be a chance to let the other fly without hindrance because you gave her the chance to see what was inside her own instincts.

8

Resisting the Cs: Changing and Controlling Your Mother or Daughter

Blythe

Sunday mornings used to be so easy. I would lay out their clothes, put the kids in the bathtub, towel dry them, and dress them; and when they could dress themselves, show them the cute clothes I picked out, and they would wear them. Then as their clothes sizes started to grow, so did their independence and tastes. Soon I got vetoed in my choices of clothing for Sunday-morning church. The cute outfits—still hanging in the closet. The pretty shoes—still lined up from the last time I put them in the closet.

I've had to let go of control and trying to change my daughters regarding their clothes. And not just on Sunday mornings, but on other occasions as well. I see the nicer clothes we've bought and I want them to wear those. They would look so cute, and yes, I think how they dress reflects on me as the mom. How could a parent let her daughters wear bicycle shorts to church?

Yes, that actually happened…when I was on a trip. My husband and kids picked me up from the airport after they went to church. One of my girls was wearing a Star Wars T-shirt and bicycle shorts. I cringed. I winced. I wondered what people thought of me for letting my daughter wear that to church. If only they had known it wasn't my fault—I was out of town! My lack of control bothered me. I eventually gave it up. My wanting to change them to want to wear the "proper" outfits showed me I cared more about their physical appearance than their hearts.

As I battled this for some Sundays before I finally let them choose their own outfits, it seemed to me the message I was sending was this: You have to be dressed up to go meet with God. Ugh. That is not at all what I want them to remember about church. I want them to know that they have a unique contribution to make, and that their individual personalities are what contribute to God's people, not how they look. It's not easy to refrain from saying something and to try not to change their appearance so others will be impressed that I took the time to have well-dressed children. But ultimately I care more about how I come across to my children than I do others, so this is a good reminder of where to focus my attention. It took some time for me to get to this place, but I feel more freedom just by taking the pressure off them.

Change may or may not be a word we typically embrace. Change jobs, change homes, change the channel. It denotes you're leaving something in search of something new.

Sometimes it's not your choice to change, and it is presented to you that if you don't change this, you'll lose that. Or if you can't change, then you're not an agreeable person. When someone tries to change who you are or how you live, do you bristle a bit? Right behind this comes the other *C* word: *control.* How easy it is to want control, but how hard it is when we are on the receiving end. Are we right or right?!

Would you recognize control in your life if someone asked you if you're a controlling person? We tend to think we aren't controlling but that we just have a strong opinion or desire to have some say on the outcome of a situation. But what's more accurate is that sometimes we tend to want to control or change the other person, and our actions have gone beyond asking if we can give feedback (as we saw in the previous chapter) and we are now trying to control or change the other person. Our control is other-centered, but how often do we look at our self-control? There's a verse in Proverbs that says, "Like a city that is broken into and without walls is a man who has no control over his spirit" (25:28).

Not many strong-willed women want to self-identify that they don't have self-control over their spirit and words to another. This leads us to think about what kind of control we are after—our own self-control or our control over another's life? Deep pause.

Helen

Trying to change your mother or your daughter is like praying for rain in a desert. No one likes a controlling person, and we'll look further into how control actually comes from fear and feeling a lack of control. You want to have breathing room in the relationship without control. Acceptance of one another and letting go are such gifts to the relationship.

Blythe

Earlier I mentioned I felt freedom when I let go of trying to change and control what my daughters wore. I thought I had control, but when I backed off I felt more in control of *me* because I was free. I realized I was emotionally healthier because of it.

Helen

Praying for restoration in your emotional and relational health can lead to both great and terrible "aha" moments. These realizations first came for me when, as we shared in chapter 2, Blythe left home for college. The changes I was experiencing went way beyond the normal emotional range of adjusting to not having either of my children under my roof anymore. I was desperate to have more control, and as I looked deeper into the cause of that desperation, God began to clear things up for me.

A huge piece of the puzzle is that I was looking at my relationship with Blythe out of an unfulfilled place in my heart and relationship with my mother. I was needy and didn't know it.

The word *overcheck* is used to describe the thin leather strap that's attached to a horse's bit to keep its head up. And isn't that how we often are with control of others? We are trying to ensure that their head is up, according to us, and that we have some control. Neediness (an emotional overcheck) is a real obstacle in the life of mothers and daughters—their own as well as the life of their relationship. It has tentacles that reach to other areas of the relationship and get trapped under an area of the person's control, even if it has nothing to do with them. For instance, a mother trying to control where a daughter lives may end up with a neediness to be close to her daughter and this can stifle the daughter from the potential friends, church, job, and all the things we teach them to go after. Neediness says, "I want you to be near me rather than move where there are unknown opportunities and people." The control then goes from where the daughter lives to other areas in her life.

We admittedly have basic needs to meet in various ways, but we were never intended to depend on people or circumstances to fill us up or to try to control them so that we would feel better about ourselves and the roles we play.

You've been around people you sense are "needy" emotionally and even feel the tentacles. Do you want to run or stay? Running is a good and healthy choice! We care about the person, most certainly, but the warning is about not entering into a codependent relationship. This is even more dangerous when it comes to the mother-daughter relationship. It's not a relationship we were designed to run from. It may have turned out that way for you, but it's not how it's supposed to go. I feel deeply for you if this has been your experience as it has been a part of mine. And it's a hard place to navigate, so please know my heart is for you in this.

There isn't room for codependence in a relationship where two individuals are dependent on God, not each other, to fill them up. Yet we slip into codependence and often don't realize when we are not doing what is best for us but are trying to do what's best for another person because we attach our worth to those actions.

Alcoholics Anonymous has a saying that "alcoholics don't have relationships; they take hostages." The same can be said of codependent relationships. A codependent doesn't have relationships; he or she takes hostages. It's powerful to think about, isn't it? Maybe this is how you have lived your life with your mother or daughter...or both.

Over-Love Overload

Helen

Over-love is a word I made up as I thought more about codependency. Many over-reaches made by well-intentioned mothers to "help" their beloved daughters might seem loving, but in many cases they are over-loving. It is a subtle form of control, and it feels like control to the daughter. I would say Blythe and I have a just-right love now.

The root cause of relational control is fear. Fear that something bad will happen to the person you love, fear things won't end well, or fear that things won't go like we want them to or how things "should" go.

If you've been around someone who seems to suck the air out of you, you could be with a codependent person. One of the dangers is they are attempting to get their needs met by sharing their words and perhaps time with you, which feels like they are being controlling. A second danger is that you are being pulled into their neediness. This is especially difficult if it is with your mother or daughter.

One of the conversations I had with both Blythe and her brother, Bryan, when they left for college was: "I am becoming aware of how I make way too many 'suggestions,' and I don't want to be that way—bossy, a nag, suffocating...If you hear that or sense me heading that way in the slightest, please say, 'Mom, I hear control.'" They were either too gracious or I got better, for they never shared those words with me. To date, they are welcome to tell me if they feel the tentacles of over-love. I want to have the right level of love and not control. I know they are their own independent individuals raising their own children, and I would want them to remember their years as adults as living with freedom.

Obviously, the antidote for having tentacles is letting go. I have a fairly fat file folder of poems and articles about letting go so it's been a go-to button with me for a long time. I've taken these into my mental file folder so that if I do want to make a suggestion, I think about how best to word it.

Anger in Distance

One end of the relationship spectrum is this over-love enmeshment (too close), and on the other end is distance from your loved one. One of the factors that creates distance is anger. I would say anger has created most of the mother wounds and daughter wounds we know.

Anger is said to be our response when things aren't going the way we expect. Letting go of our hidden and overt expectations is a help. In addition to letting go of your expectations, if you have an emotional grip on your mother or daughter, can you let go of the control? Can you release her in other ways?

One thing you want to look out for in an enmeshment situation (the over-love) is enabling the other person. If you struggle with this, your form of control is to be the one who enables them to get what they want. But this is where you need to put up some boundaries. This is a difficult place to be because you may be acting out of good intentions to help them, but the results are still the same: control after you have enabled them. It's controlling them through helping them. Controlling can produce anger from the one being controlled, which can then drive distance between you. One question you can ask is: **"How do you see me helping you but not controlling?"** It's a powerful question.

Distance in the Relationship

When there is distance in your relationship, the answer to drawing closer lies perhaps in a call to prayer, a call to dialog, or a call to forgiveness (or all three). Our friend Ann has seen the power of a call to pray a prodigal back home. A prodigal is an example of distance (too far)—the opposite of enmeshment (over-love).

> I was invited by Helen to come to Dalton, Georgia, to speak at a ladies event at a church. During the ministry time that day, I heard the Lord say, "Now, call in the prodigals." Phew! Not accustomed to doing this type of ministry, I hesitated. Then I heard, "Do it!" So I just obeyed. "Anyone who has a prodigal, please come forward." I spoke out thinking there must be a huge group that needed this. Two women came forward. One of the women was shaking and crying, obviously upset. She told of the loss of her daughter. Then I called her prodigal daughter home. I took a deep breath and yelled out to her daughter at the top of my lungs: "JESSICA! Get up from the dark place…turn around and start heading home. Come in the front door of your mother's house." That was it. I delivered the request of the Lord.
>
> The next day about suppertime Helen called excited and exuberant. "Ann, Jessica just came home!" She came through the *front door* of her mother's house. You don't understand. Her mother has one of those long walkways leading to the street. Jessica would have driven around to the back ordinarily, but she came home to the front door after being away for a year and a half.

It is never too late to pray for a prodigal, whether it's been years or months. God may use you or someone else to call them home. But taking the step to pray or enlist others to pray with the belief that God will answer is a good first step. What a powerful story this is to show that God wants us to cry out to Him and that He answers our prayers.

If you have a prodigal, you know strong prayer is needed. One of the most important roles of mothers and daughters is that of intercessors. The most common model is a mother praying for a prodigal daughter. But there are many daughters who pray for their mothers. You may want to ask, here and now, "Where is there a rift in my relationship with my mother or daughter? God, show me what I'm to do in order to restore the foundation that was created between us by You."

A prayer for the prodigal you may wish to pray now would include these things:

1. Welcoming God's presence
2. Giving yourself to Him and coming under His authority
3. Placing His authority over your heart
4. Asking for clarity
5. Praying for the prodigal to come home
6. Restoring you to each other

Or if you would like a more constructed prayer, here is one to consider praying:

> Lord, You see those of us in the faraway places. Your eye is always upon us. I know You see my prodigal (daughter/mother). With the authority I have as Your child, I ask You to bring her home. I call _____ (insert name) home today in the name of the Lord Jesus. I pray for every need she has and for Your plan for interventions in her life, to bring her to Yourself. I believe these mended needs are part of her healing. I trust You and Your timing, Lord,

and in my heart bow before You to Your sovereignty in my life and her life and our relationship. May Your ways be accomplished for her and may Your Spirit overshadow her and bring her home in a true physical sense and spiritually to You, breaking the power of where she has been. Light over darkness. I pray for repentance and rest. Isaiah 30:15 says, "For thus the Lord GOD, the Holy One of Israel, has said, 'In repentance and rest you will be saved, in quietness and trust is your strength.'" In the name of my Lord and Savior, I bring Your banner over me and my loved one to return home.

After you pray this, you may need to discern what else is missing. God can reveal even more as we come to Him in prayer. It's possible there are other things you don't have at the top of your mind that need to come to the surface or have forgotten about, and when all of this does surface, it helps you move forward in wholeness.

Maybe you don't have a prodigal who has left you physically but a daughter or mother who has left you emotionally. You will still want to pray a prayer with the intention of returning to each other so that you can be restored and move into the next important stage of reconciliation: repairing breaches between you.

Repairing Breaches

Helen

There are many land mines in families, but we can learn to navigate them. God has called us to repair the breaches (Isaiah 58:12). In Isaiah's time there was a breach in the ways that men and women lived their lives since the time their ancestors looked to Abraham and Moses. These men and women did not live according to the laws of God and His plans for them, and it was a mess! After God wiped out generations and the idols that entangled them, He told the people He would bring restoration back. He is the one who can repair the breaches that we have brought on ourselves or walked through because of someone else's actions.

The repair begins with recognizing there's a breach, and then asking for God to come and show us our part of the breach. We are not responsible for fixing the other person's part of the breach, although there is much we can do on our end to pray and have an open hand toward the other person as God leads.

A common behavioral principle is that whomever we focus on, we will emulate and become like that person. This is why and how unhealthy family patterns begin. Maybe you've heard the old adage, "Be careful what you think about concerning your mother-in-law or you'll become just like her!" The same could be said of your mother. If we focus too much on her and what we wish to change, we could easily end up repeating the patterns we focus on.

This is why Blythe and I wanted to write this book—to show you don't have to repeat the patterns that have been set before you. I had to choose a different way to raise Blythe and her brother, and she has had to think about how she wanted to raise her children differently from the generations before her. Making new tracks is what this message is about—repairing the tracks before you where you can and making new ones for your family where you are now.

Maybe this confirms your belief that you need to do things separately from the generations before you, and up until now you haven't really seen it as a choice you get to make, to carve your own path. But you aren't sure how to do this, especially when your parenting is all you've known. You're aware the worn path you've walked with your mother isn't what you want your daughter to tread. It may take some digging to really ask, "Where do I want to take a different path with my daughter than what was done for me?"

Do you sense that you're repeating a pattern anywhere? Some patterns we repeat without realizing it—how we speak to our daughters, how we prioritize their importance, and such. If your mother has abusive speech, you as a daughter are at risk for repeating that pattern. If there is or has been physical abuse in the home, you need to share with someone in authority to get help. Maybe your mother didn't come to your defense when you were abused or she was the abuser. This could be the enormous chasm or breach that is between you. Perhaps she knew about a person who violated you or she doesn't know and you are withholding this from her. These are of great concern and need to be addressed because you will not fully have access to your mother's heart, and she yours, without these areas being brought into the light. A child of the Light can't stay in the dark. Jesus tells us He is the Light of the world. John 8:12 says, "Then Jesus again spoke to them, saying, 'I am the Light of the world; he who follows Me will not walk in the darkness, but will have the Light of life.'"

Often it's easier to keep what's in the dark there. It seems safer not to expose what we wish happened or didn't happen in our relationship. Bringing anything to the Light that you sense needs addressing with each other requires a deeper healing and intervention between you that we will address in this chapter, and in the next chapter we will look at generational patterns and prayers you will want to pray.

You will also want to enlist the help of a reputable Christian counselor to help you process these areas with deeper healing. It's so important to dive deep into abuse and issues that have come from control. There absolutely can be forgiveness between you as mother and daughter even in these circumstances. But it can't happen if it stays hidden. So that's why we encourage you to think about how you can bring this up with your mother/daughter and with a counselor to help you process this together. The health that can come for your relationship and any others you are mothering in your family can have a rippling effect or a crippling effect if not addressed.

If you believe this is true, how does this change your past as you dream about a new future? Where can you start repairing breaches between you and look at how you want to live differently?

Seeing Your Own Land Mine

Helen

Do you remember how we talked about two relational spectrums and land mines in families? One was over-love and the other was distance. I was on the spectrum of distance. My mom's anger did distance me. I was on the defense much of the time. Her anger was also combined with control. There were many land mines for sure, but God taught me much, and the big takeaway was the deep desire not to repeat the pattern with my own children. But because I was very focused on her anger, having stuffed and neglected my own issues, I was at high risk for repeating her pattern. God did intervene years later to break the possibility of that pattern being repeated, helping me see that I was too over-loving with Blythe! That was my "aha" moment!

Blythe

Okay, it's only fair for me to insert myself here. I didn't feel an over-love from Mom. I didn't know she felt like she was gripping me. I felt like a loved kid whose parents paid attention to me and cared about the things I cared about. But it's interesting that Mom felt like she was over-loving me. You can see that our perspective sometimes isn't what the other feels. I do remember my senior year of high school wanting to spread my wings more, and I know I distanced myself from Mom some. It's possible I could have felt over-love then. I was also going through a hard year of having my brother away at college and navigating my senior year with less interest than I had in previous school years. So often I would distance myself from Mom and others, which might have caused her to feel like she was over-loving. See how important these things are to talk about? You don't always know what your mother or daughter is thinking, and it's so helpful to talk about it while it's happening, rather than waiting to do so years later.

Helen

I thank you, Blythe, for that. It does help to know what is running through the minds of both mothers and daughters. Do you see more closely how talking is a barometer of the relationship?

I wish I had known to have a deeper conversation with my mom during the years of her anger and control. It always seemed hard to have a conversation with her about her anger. I never wanted to upset her further, but I wish I'd said more or written more. I believe I was kind to her, but I wish I had known to see more clearly her issues, my issues, and our issues together—and speak of them!

We all respond to hurt, trauma, abuse, and the like in different ways. My unhealthy but routine response was to internalize and say little. It wasn't denial—it was just the only way I knew how to respond at that time.

This is again why I am so passionate about our seeking what issues God would have us deal with and learning how to speak up in conversation with the person involved, whether that's your mother or daughter. For situations that would prove to be physically or emotionally risky to share in person, you can write. If you feel you might be misunderstood or misinterpreted, it is good to write out the conversation of how you don't want to change the person but you want to address what's occurred between you. We know we cannot change another person or what's between us, but we can submit our control, and we can submit our desire to try to change someone. We do this by daily choosing the route of stepping back versus trying to master control of the other.

Fear is usually at the root of a controlling person. The controller is controlling situations because she feels as though things won't turn out the way she wants them to (she has a set goal of what she'd like to see). But a controlling parent puts fear in the relationship.

If you are ready to speak to your mother or daughter to address the control you feel or the desire you have to change the other, here is a possible conversation starter for you:

> Mom, we're in a tangle, aren't we? I believe both of us want a good relationship, but we have some obstacles. Help me to understand your anger with me…I want to understand…I want us to do well…I see your pain…I want us to be restored…What do you think we need to do to make things better?

You want to be guided by the Spirit of God in your wording and timing, but these words might serve as a guide for either a verbal or written conversation. As you seek Him, He will show you when you are to speak and when you are to be silent and wait for the right time.

One of the other reasons I love questions (the what-do-you-think kind) is that questions help us not to control by giving advice straight out of the gate! Questions can be misused, however. When the question is invasive, controlling, nagging, or punitive in any way, the question will not help mend the relationship. It will have the opposite effect.

The questions we've inserted in this book as suggested conversations are meant to be gentle, loving, humble, honest, and earnest clarifiers. That's what can bring health to relationships and personal freedom to you.

There's one more tentacle to name. My deep desire to connect with my mom despite her anger led to an unhealthy fixation. I thought about her constantly—wondering where the next land mine would be, wondering what I should do next, and focusing on her in a way that was not healthy. You can see how I was setting myself up for disaster. Unhealthy ties come as a result of enmeshment, codependency, and focusing so much on another that you virtually become one with him or her on an emotional level. You can see and feel the tentacles. You can see the unhealthy over-love. What may seem loving (like thinking about someone a lot) isn't always loving or healthy. Proverbs 14:12

says, "There is a way which *seems* right to a man, but its end is the way of death" (emphasis added).

It may seem right to fixate on how not to become like your mother or how not to mess up your relationship with your daughter, but this can become an idol and an unhealthy bond. If you've never really left your mother in the sense of claiming your own life and your own family (as Blythe was sharing about in the previous chapter) and come out from underneath the connection you made that is unhealthy, you won't experience the freedom you are meant to have as mother and daughter.

Blythe and I have both taken steps to do this, and we are healthier for it. She is not unhealthily tied to me, and I am not tied to her or my mother. In looking at control and how it can be measured in your life, I realized a couple of things that are important for you to note as well.

Mom's control was not overt—if I made a decision she didn't like or did something she didn't like, she would rage. She was attempting to control me after the fact through her anger. It was hard walking on eggshells, never knowing what would set her off.

It would be helpful for you to keep a journal of the control you see or feel. Doing this can guide you to know you are not minimizing what has happened or is happening to you now. And writing down your experiences will allow you to recall them so that when you do talk with your mother or daughter, you can reference them without having to try to remember and bring up details you've pushed aside or forgotten.

Blythe

One final piece as you're becoming more aware of what it looks like when you try to change or control your daughter. Trying to control or change things is generally done out of fear. The opposite of fear is confidence and courage.

We do need to be aware of what our children are up against and proactively look out for them to make sure they are safe. But when you start trying to change your daughter's surroundings and control the outcome of a situation so she doesn't get hurt, or trying to keep her from or push her into certain social settings because you don't want to expose her or leave her out—it shows a lack of confidence in her. And our daughters are smart and can pick up on it. Let's commit to living bravely and courageously in front of our daughters and not out of a lack of control or because of fear in our lives. Some of our favorite verses that speak to this are:

- Be strong and courageous, do not be afraid or tremble at them, for the LORD your God is the one who goes with you. He will not fail you or forsake you (Deuteronomy 31:6).

- Have I not commanded you? Be strong and courageous! Do not tremble or be dismayed, for the LORD your God is with you wherever you go (Joshua 1:9).

- Be on the alert, stand firm in the faith, act like men, be strong (1 Corinthians 16:13).

Mending Thread

Do you have a balanced approach of love for your daughter or mother? Not too controlling but not too distant? When you tend to over-love, your relationship becomes more about maintenance than creating something meaningful. It is exhausting to keep up with. A good relationship between you should be one that is natural and takes time and effort (good work!) but not one that creates a feeling of being overwhelmed.

God doesn't control us, and we weren't meant to control our children or our mother. A daughter shouldn't use her role to control if or when her mother has access to her or her children. There should be mutual respect, not a mutual trying to change the other or control the other. You want to submit, to bow to the other. But how do you do this if it's a difficult relationship?

You are her mother or daughter, not the person she gets to walk over. You get to decide what's healthy for you as you talk with her about it. While you don't want to intentionally withhold from her, you also don't want to run over her with your controlling words and actions. You will want to work out the balance so that it's a fair arrangement for you both.

Making It Personal: Praying Over Control and Strongholds

Many mothers and daughters may recognize degrees of codependency, over-love, and enmeshment in their relationship. It is a good thing to recognize these boundary-violation issues and seek the right source for repair. Sadly, often the missing piece of the recovery is praying off these ties. Taking your authority as a believer and praying are of huge importance if these strongholds are there. Or you may have prayed off these strongholds but have needed further counsel. Ask the Lord what you need and seek it. You want to close off anything that you have possibly let back in that has not given you the effective tools to continue in this battle for recovery of your relationship.

If you want a prayer to pray off these relationship strongholds, here is one:

> Father God, I see that I have put my relationship with
> _____ in too high a place and that it is
> a detriment to my own emotional life as well as my spiritual life with You. It is idolatry, unhealthy, and a substitute for Your Spirit in me. I repent. I now pray off this unhealthy alliance by breaking every enmeshment and unhealthy relationship with _____ and ask for Your Spirit to refill the empty spaces left now. May I not seek substitutes. Lord, may You lead me and guide me into healthier relationships, particularly with my mother/daughter.

Breaking the unhealthy alliance you have with your mother or daughter in this way is a pivotal place to separate your life from hers and your thinking from hers. First Timothy 1:5 says, "But the goal of our instruction is love from a pure heart and a good conscience and a sincere faith." This should be our goal when we consider how we love our mother or daughter and what our motives are in our relationship. Paul was telling Timothy to stay true to God's work, which is faith. And if we are going to enter into a new place in our faith with God for our mother or daughter, it is appropriate to seal it with a pure heart and a good conscience moving forward.

How does what we have uncovered in this chapter change how you see that you are either too connected to your mother or daughter or appropriately connected to her? Does this bring about clarity to make a change? We hope so and encourage you to take this step, because the freedom you gain in not just your relationship with each other but in the rest of your life is immeasurable! Freedom is free, but you have to grab hold of it.

9

A New Generation: Setting Things Differently

In the past couple of years, tracing your generational ancestry has become the thing to do. Looking at your bloodline and even the type of genetic makeup you have has become trendy. Maybe you have traced your ancestry to a country you didn't even know was in your lineage and suddenly you want to vacation there and learn more about your surname. But how often do we look at the spiritual factors of our generational makeup?

We believe that praying through generational patterns and family actions and replacing and establishing new healthy patterns are the most important elements for you as a mother or daughter to begin to see things differently in your family.

It's true that what we've experienced is often tied to the generation before us. And their words or actions have opened a door to who we believe we are. But under the covering of Jesus, it's not the truth of who we are.

"The stories from our past that shaped us and the words that were spoken over our lives that have crippled us do not stand a chance in the light of the powerful grace and mercy that come to us now in the

Person of Jesus. We do not have to remain captive any longer," says Stasi Eldredge in her book *Becoming Myself: Embracing God's Dream of You.*[1] "It's easy to blame our mothers. Children will blame their moms when they are hurt (so will teenagers)."[2]

How do we look at what we have inherited from the generations before us and separate ourselves from it? A good place to start is by acknowledging what is or has been a difficult place in your life and being willing to say how it has hurt you and affected your ability to be a daughter and/or mother.

Helen

My relationship with my mother was so difficult it was hard to even buy a Mother's Day card or a birthday card. I wasn't going to send a card saying things that weren't true. I wanted to stay honest and true to my own emotions, but I was committed to respecting her position in my life. I didn't want to shame her by not sending a card. What helped me was remembering that *she wasn't who she wanted to be either*. She wasn't well. Her anger and anxieties weren't healed yet, and so, in a sense, she was a victim too. God gave me love and compassion beyond measure in those times. I didn't know much then about breaking generational ties, but something in me knew I didn't want Blythe to ever feel that way.

Blythe told you a little about my mother in the first chapter, and I've talked about how on edge I felt around her and her anger toward me. And the unhealthy relationship I had with her is largely how this generational pattern played out for me.

Today is my mom's birthday, so I am doing a lot of reflecting…again. She died in 1998, but I am still flooded with memories. Mostly they are good ones, but the bad ones sure did some damage. God is still healing my heart as He does, in layers like filo pastry. There are outer layers that come off more easily, but sometimes the ones underneath are harder to navigate.

I need to share her story with you because this is why Blythe and I are writing about mending and restoring the heart. The difficult chapters in my story with my mom could have become my story with Blythe because generational sins and patterns are real and repeat themselves. So for decades we have purposed to uncover and heal from any unhealthy patterns as well as not repeat them in our family's new generations. With God's help we have hopefully shattered those patterns forever! It is so redemptive to have a good relationship when you haven't. Through recognizing what's unhealthy there can be growth and change. People don't mature when there's not difficulty. In seeing what I experienced with my mom, it gave me the desire not only to change but to make a new way for my own family. Over the years we have grown in our understanding of how to break off generational issues and how to daily give our lives to the work of Christ in us as we come under His authority.

It is the purpose of my heart to give my mom the respect she deserves as I share about her life and my understanding of how to navigate a different life for my children. I think she would even be glad that her emotional pain could be useful and helpful for others. She was like that. As I share about her, it is not meant as a complaint, whining, or disrespect. It is meant to paint an honest picture of the patterns we needed help with to change our future. Some who know us may be shocked because I haven't shared much over the years about my mom's issues and our often very difficult relationship. I still grieve at the loss of her and miss her so much. I grieve that we didn't mend as much as we could have before she died. I also grieve that she didn't receive the help she needed for her own peace before she died.

Last, I grieve that there is a trace of relief that the drama is over. I wish that wasn't there, but I had protected my own heart and the ears and hearts of my family for so long. The day-to-day drama was gone, but what remained were patterns we focused on and thereby ran the risk of repeating. For again, whatever you focus on, you run the risk of repeating. And this is the underpinning of generational patterns we want to break so that they don't move past your experience and into the lives of those behind you.

These might be the hardest set of paragraphs I've written in this whole book. Please hear the love, and please hear our need to heal.

As I look around my home, I see things in every single room that my mother provided. I am grateful for her thoughtfulness and generosity. She had a huge heart for giving gifts to her family and friends. It gave her so much joy. She was brilliant. She was a great administrator and planner and made lists like crazy. She was a fun person and gregarious, had a beautiful singing voice, and was a leader among her friends. Many called her daily. She loved sports and was most outspoken about her teams. She took losses of her teams pretty hard. Mom had a privileged upbringing, and I have wondered often if that's one reason why disappointments were hard for her.

But when something didn't go right, her anger went over the top. Mostly it was toward me, my dad, and her mom. There was a part of me that knew we were her safe place, but it also hurt. It was verbal and emotional abuse, and I knew it was unhealthy for all of us.

Her assaulting words to me were things like, "You can never do anything right" and "You are so stupid." Constant criticism. Constant control. I walked on eggshells, afraid to defend myself or retaliate. I wanted her love, approval, and acceptance so much—too much! I would learn about healthy boundaries later, but I didn't know about them at the time.

She had social anxiety. Strangely, she was drawn to a social life, but also feared she wasn't enough. So she drank to feel more relaxed, and thus began her dependency on alcohol. Years of denial followed and then treatment. All the while her anger was untreated. She cared too much about appearances but failed to see her public and explosive anger as outside the normal range. It was a puzzle that she cared so much what others thought but seemed oblivious to how she looked when ranting. Or how it affected those of us in her path.

She was unpredictable. She would greet me with nurturing open arms, and in minutes be angry if something wasn't right in her world. It was a long season of feeling unsafe emotionally. I never remember feeling safe with Mom, even when she would hug me. When we would arrive at her and Dad's home with my husband and children, there would be a warm greeting, but then it wouldn't take long before she'd be upset about something. Every visit I hoped things would be different, which was pretty naive of me because nothing had changed. She hadn't changed, and I hadn't changed. How were we going to experience a change in our relationship?

It felt as though she was with her friends more than she was with me. She was emotionally unavailable. When life got hard, Mom couldn't handle it, perhaps. Her life had been soft and easy. It was difficult to understand why she wouldn't move toward me when she seemed to love other things and people in life.

All the while it was also scary wondering if I would replicate her anger and control with my own children. I also felt great shame and embarrassment when my children heard or saw her episodes. I knew she also was depressed and had fear in her life. Anger is a signal that you didn't get what you expected, that things are not like you want them to be.

I longed for peace during those many years of tears. Even up to her last hours on this earth, I also longed for her happiness. She was in the hospital and facing surgery and asked if I would go to the nearby mall and purchase some pajamas. I was thrilled to have the assignment, still anxious to please her. (God has had to do a lot of surgery there. I sadly turned into a people pleaser and needed His help greatly.) I found the Barbizon pajamas she loved and also found something she had talked about often: black velvet flat shoes with jewels on them. My heart was soaring. I could hardly wait to give them to her! So, bounding into the hospital room, I gave her the pajamas and the flats. Her response was anger—the flats didn't have the right kind of heel. That was one of our last conversations before she died. Yes, I know she was probably scared and took it out on me and the black velvet shoes, but that is how unwell we were.

We didn't understand it, but we knew some things were terribly wrong. Ultimately, Mom became the gift that helped us begin to get healthier as individuals and as a family. We were strong believers, including my mom, but there were some big gaps.

One of the first things that brought some clarity about the dysfunctions in our family was a pamphlet I came across entitled "Children of Confusion." It's similar to material for children of alcoholics. On one page was a description of much of what I was walking through. Soon thereafter I began graduate studies in counseling, and pertinent information began to come tumbling forth. God was so faithful to help me see one issue after another for our family's healing. It wasn't that God's Word and His principles weren't enough, or that His Spirit couldn't direct me. I had buried myself in Bible studies for the previous 28 years of Mom's life. I just needed even more resources on the specific topic to go deeper. I didn't want to mask my issues and appear okay just because I was a believer. I knew I needed repair in my life and wanted to get well. One of the most important things Blythe and I wanted to share from what we've seen and experienced is this: how to mend relationships as you identify and then make new generational patterns.

Blythe

I don't remember a time my mom showed anger or yelled or did anything less than hug me and affirm me. It is unbelievable to me that the loving mom I grew up with could have been exposed to what she was exposed to and be the amazing mom she has been during my life. I never remember feeling as though I was anything but truly valued and loved for who I was. I felt safe, nurtured, and protected. Mom started a new generation; she set things differently.

And I thought, naively, that all kids felt this way. It wasn't until college that I realized not everyone grew up the way I did. I lived in a normal that didn't exist for most. I assumed everyone had the kind of mother I had. And I didn't fully understand what she had gone through, as I only really knew what life was like for my mom when she was an adult.

Often I would wonder how my grandfather could continue to live under the pressure of his wife getting angry. His faithful love to her taught me a lot about the power of love. And it hurt me to see my grandmother getting angry at my mom when we were together. I remember hiding in her house once when I was little and being upset that my mom had to hear such words. I remember trying to love my mom as much as I could to make up for what she was hearing from her mom.

I know now, as I creep toward mid-life, I was spared and richly blessed and given something so rare that many children don't experience: unconditional love.

But look how God has restored. Mom is a mother to so many people. She has a mothering spirit where they haven't been mothered. She still meets people who tell her, "You are like the mother I didn't have." She loves so expansively, so fully, and she is the most generous giver. I am thankful to have been taught all my life that I am so loved for who I am.

Andrew Wommack says in his book *Don't Limit God,*

> Some children are told from a young age that they aren't wanted or that they will never amount to anything…When we believe the negative words or ideas that are spoken over us, it forms an image on the inside of us of who we are and what we can do. That image serves as a ceiling that we can't rise above. Even though our talents and abilities could take us further, we don't allow them to.[3]

Wommack believes we have to "change the image on the inside of us and start seeing ourselves through God's Word."[4]

It's easy, from what I understand from Mom, to believe the words spoken over you. Things like, "You're a zero" or "You're not doing it right," or whatever it may be that threatens you. It would seem like hot water poured on a heart that is trying to hang on. It scorches and hurts. Charles Spurgeon said, "A lie can travel halfway around the world while the truth is putting on its shoes." I imagine it was easy for Mom and perhaps for you to look at the lies that were poured on you and see those rather than what sometimes takes longer to see: the truth.

What would the truth look like in those situations? If we were to ask you to go back to those scenes in your mind, what were the lies? What do you more accurately see as the truth back then? And do you recognize it as truth in your life now? You are not held back or taken out by the words of others if you know how to replace them with what God offers you. And you are the one to stand in the breach of what was taken from you and stop it so that it doesn't continue into future generations. You are the generational stopgap—it doesn't have to go any further, and you are the key to dialing it back and out of your family at this stage.

Strongholds

Helen

> For though we walk in the flesh, we do not war according to the flesh, for the weapons of our warfare are not of the flesh, but divinely powerful for the destruction of fortresses. We are destroying speculations and every lofty thing raised up against the knowledge of God, and we are taking every thought captive to the obedience of Christ (2 Corinthians 10:3-5).

Generational patterns can create strongholds, which is why it's so important to set things differently for your family. According to these verses, the key to overcoming strongholds is bringing every thought captive. A stronghold is a worn place of defeat. When you entertain a thought or act it out and start living with it at the center of your life, it becomes a stronghold. For me and my mom, the stronghold became how I lived with a lower value of my life and in fear of what she could do to me with her words and actions. My anxiety fed into this stronghold that I wouldn't be a good mother and might turn out to be like the one who had caused me so much pain. Because of what I saw in their relationship, I assume I was probably reliving what my mom lived with her mother. After I became a Christian at age 27 right before Blythe was born, God started preparing me to pour out His wisdom on my children and stop the pattern from continuing.

What has occurred in your mother-daughter relationship (and any others you are aware of before yours) needs to be brought before the Father as you ask Him for clarity and guidance on what you need to break away from and begin a new path of belief. It could even be a negative message you think you've heard but wasn't really from your mom. But there's a stronghold between you. You aren't hearing it from her but from the enemy of your heart. Satan is a schemer and wants you to think less of yourself than you really are. Often if a thought comes into your mind, and if it's not something that you know comes from our heavenly Father, it has come from the deceiver, who makes it seem as though it's what your mother or daughter thinks. You want to get this thought out in the open and release your mother or daughter from it and address it with her.

You may be the mom who sees your daughter as the object of your choices and you feel as though you'll never be what she should have had as a mom. But it's a stronghold not coming from your daughter— it's a place in your heart you've piled on words of remorse that have created a false sense of you as a mother. You want to release this and not let this stronghold take you captive from the life you want with your daughter.

God's goal for us is freedom. Galatians 5:1 says, "It was for freedom that Christ set us free; therefore keep standing firm and do not be subject again to a yoke of slavery." The freedom that comes from naming and releasing generational patterns in your life will surprise you with how you are able to more easily navigate your life as a mother or daughter. It sets you up to live with peace over your life. You no longer feel under a yoke of slavery to the person who has created the generational patterns you have recognized. It may be a dad or grandfather who instigated the generational issues you or your mom were born into. Separation between mothers and daughters, divorce, abuse, neglect, and other issues can be passed down from generation to generation. This could also include addiction, dependency, bondage to substances, or any form of a stronghold toward something to fill you other than the Trinity: God the Father, Jesus, His Son, and the Holy Spirit.

There are a number of verses explaining that there are generational issues we need to be aware of as followers of Jesus. We are listing some below with a few more in appendix B for you to use in your own personal study.

....

Then the LORD passed by in front of him and proclaimed, "The LORD, the LORD God, compassionate and gracious, slow to anger, and abounding in lovingkindness and truth; who keeps lovingkindness for thousands, who forgives iniquity, transgression and sin; yet He will by no means leave the guilty unpunished, visiting the iniquity of fathers on the children and on the grandchildren to the third and fourth generations" (Exodus 34:6-7).

But the sons of the slayers he did not put to death, according to what is written in the book of the Law of Moses, as the LORD commanded, saying, "The fathers shall not be put to death for the sons, nor the sons be put to death for the fathers; but each shall be put to death for his own sin" (2 Kings 14:6).

The person who sins will die. The son will not bear the punishment for the father's iniquity, nor will the father bear the punishment for the son's iniquity; the righteousness of the righteous will be upon himself, and the wickedness of the wicked will be upon himself (Ezekiel 18:20).

Our fathers sinned, and are no more; it is we who have borne their iniquities (Lamentations 5:7).

These verses are meant to help you see that sins can be passed down from one generation to the next, and the best way to deal with them is to pray over your family.

Praying for Your Family

Blythe

In 2012, I distinctly remember praying for the release from generational patterns in my family of origin and setting things differently for my own family. I had been married for eight years and had young children, and I was praying to put a stopgap on my previous family members' actions and choices so the patterns would not be passed down. When I got married, I had prayed to release myself from any unhealthy ties with my mom and dad as I entered my own family. But in this prayer time as a young mom, I was setting a new pattern for my children and their children and the generations to follow.

When you combine your families, it's important to do this on both sides. How do you and your spouse agree on how you want to pray over your family, not just when you marry, but throughout your married life? You want to break any generational patterns that are unhealthy that both of you have brought into the family line from the past.

Praying over your family and speaking truth about the goodness of God really pay off when your children see the impact doing this has and when they begin to pray over your family and speak words of truth like this as well. Our daughter Maris said to me during a pivotal point in Mom's chemo journey, "Pastor Luke says that when something bad happens don't worry about it. Like Nannie has surgery and you don't worry about it. You pray over it."

They hear the message of declaring what you know to be true when you say this in front of them and it sticks. Breaking away from generational patterns and setting up new patterns for your children to pray are what they will carry with them to their children. You want to pray and speak words that bring healing and understanding over your child so that your family can walk in a generation of faithfulness.

Breaking Off Lies You Believe

Helen

We've talked about strongholds as worn places of defeat and how to remove these from your thought life. Another area you'll want to detach from is lies or messages that have been passed down to you (such as I did with my mom's rants). You want to ask Jesus to cleanse and break the power of these lies. They could be anything from your not being wanted in your family to how you brought shame upon the family or caused divisions to take place in the family or any other lie that feels true.

If lies like these reside in your heart and you do not commit them to prayer, issues such as anger, control, or living your life without the power of God will develop and grow. There is an authority over us beyond our mother, and God is that authority who has the power to defeat anything in your life. Your mom can't do it for you, and she may have, in some ways, created your pain. You can't expect her to heal you, nor should you. But God, through the person of Jesus, has defeated all of the darkness you face, and He alone is able to redeem your life and the lives of the family you are a part of and are creating.

My daughter-in-law, Lynn, has been a strong giver of words and prayers to Blythe and me as we wrote this book. She is a deep ally with us and has discerningly shared,

> Through the power of repentance and our faith with confessions you can repent of the sin revealed by the Holy Spirit, apply the blood of Jesus, and speak the truth to close the door on ungodly patterns...Examples of generational patterns are...unforgiveness to others or yourself, fear and anxiety, shame and guilt.
>
> Just as wounds flow through family lines, we need to be encouraged that blessings also flow generationally. God blesses offspring and descendants. As hearts are mended blessings follow.
>
> This is a powerful promise once we do pray and repent of generational strongholds: "For I will pour out water on the thirsty land and streams on the dry ground; I will pour out my Spirit on your offspring, and my blessing on your descendants" (Isaiah 44:3 ESV).

The promises of a faithful generation are ours to participate in, and God speaks clearly about this. It is something every family should want to experience, but not all know of its importance. Often we think of what's right in front of us, but we need to look at what has gone on before us and how to set the course for the legacy of faith behind us.

Mending Thread

You might not have realized that the things you have experienced or held on to in your family line have had the power over your life that they have. For many people this is new territory to address. We have learned there is a lot we can do and have done in looking at our individual words and relationships. But there is even more we need to take careful evaluation of in our family line, and we believe the same will be essential for you too. A prayer to break generational patterns is shared below to get you started:

> Father God, in the name, power, authority, and shed blood of Jesus I pray off all generational strongholds in my family. I pray to the tearing down of these generational patterns: sins from my mother's and father's family lines, addiction, vows that have been made to others and to entities that are outside of my control. I recognize and put an end to the damaging behaviors passed down through my family line that I will not allow to continue in my generation. I receive the blood covering of Jesus who has made me the righteousness of God in Christ.

Making It Personal: Drawing Your Family Line and Erasing Lies

Make a generational drawing of your family with some of the identifying issues you don't wish to repeat.

If you were to make a family tree, what would it include of the issues in your family? This will allow you to see the patterns of those who had anxiety, fear, destructive behaviors, and more—and how they have affected you.

Ask the Holy Spirit to show you unhealed places in your identity and watch for what He highlights. Often there is a lie of some type of lack in your life that you've made an agreement with and believe is true of you. It could be a lack of self-worth, a lack of the ability to be loved, a lack of boundaries, or another lack you now perceive in your adult years. You can then confess that lie and repent for your part in agreeing with the lie. This breaks off the power of the lie, as does declaring the truth of who you are as a daughter of the King.

What is the lie of lack in your life?

What do you think about or worry about most?

How does knowing about strongholds help you to get out of a cycle of beliefs that aren't yours to carry anymore?

In prayer, you can cancel every assignment of darkness and call forth the righteous inheritance of blessings from the generations that have come before you (Deuteronomy 7:7-10). This will be a powerful new beginning for you and your family!

10

Restoring Your Heart

Helen

Ever catch on to the trend of restoring old furniture—making something new out of something that otherwise feels not as useful or as pretty to fix your eyes on? Even though Blythe and I haven't done this like many women are doing these days, we have restored our hearts. And we want to tell you about what we have seen and what doing this can mean for you. It goes deeper than just making something look good on the outside.

As we work through layers of our relationship with our mother or daughter and restore hearts, we need to become even more restored to God concerning our own heart. There are two kinds of restoration of the heart: toward God and then toward others.

Again, Proverbs 4:23 reminds us that we have issues: "Watch over your heart with all diligence, for from it flow the springs [issues] of life." It is smart to continue to go before the Lord with our need for personal restoration as well as our need for restoration with others, such as your mother or daughter.

What personal restoration looks like is deeply varied. You probably have your own favorite way to get quiet before the Lord and invite His presence. Here are some that are probably on your list:

- Listening to worship songs and singing them to Him

- Quiet seeking, listening, inviting His presence

- Reading Bible verses and praying them back to Him

- Asking Him to show anything dividing you that you might confess it

- Praying to walk in His Spirit

- Asking to walk in His love, wisdom, and direction

- Praying for the concerns on your heart

- Thanking Him for restoring your heart and helping you repair breaches and build bridges in your family

We are the most whole and restored when we are restored in our relationship with God. Then when the fractured relationships around us begin to mend, restoration occurs on a human level. This is an extra bonus, for restoration with God is premium. Restoration with God fills us with the fruit of the Spirit and gives us the love, joy, and peace needed for us to pour into our personal relationships.

One of the most essential parts of restoring our hearts toward God is to make sure we have invited Jesus into our lives as Lord and Savior. I meet so many women who did something as a child toward God such as walk down the aisle of a church or they were baptized as an infant, but they can't remember if they ever really invited Jesus into their lives. So, if you're not sure if you have, you'll want to pray a prayer something like this:

> God, I'm not fully certain whether I've invited Christ into my life to be the One I follow rather than my own ways. So right now—with understanding—I do invite Jesus to be my Savior and Lord, and I can now say that today my salvation is settled and complete. I am restored

to You. Thank You for paying for my life through the blood of Your Son, Jesus, dying on the cross for me, and I receive Him into my life today.

This starts you on a new path of restoration. Restoration with people was never meant to satisfy us and bring the fullness we have with God. Throughout the book we have given words to hopefully help mend broken relationships and restore hearts with mothers and daughters. A summary of restoring would be this: In restoring your heart with a mother or daughter, you first want to ask God to help you know what the root problem is. You know something is splintered, but what exactly? God wants to give us clarity. Then you humbly ask the other person if you can take steps to be restored. If the answer is no, respect that response. But if it is yes, you'll need to own your part in the discussions that will follow.

Your job is to focus on the log in your own eye. As Matthew 7:4-5 says, "How can you say to your brother, 'Let me take the speck out of your eye,' and behold, the log is in your own eye? You hypocrite, first take the log out of your own eye, and then you will see clearly to take the speck out of your brother's eye."

Blythe

It is easier to point out what the other needs to work on. We do this with good intentions, don't we? I can make a really good case for why my way is good for my daughters, especially since my girls and I carry the same strong-willed tendencies! But doing that is not considering their needs or hearing their ideas. When did I think my way was *the* way and that I needed to be right more than I'm wrong? I am their mother, but I am not their judge. What they will remember is how I bent down and came closer to them to hear them and to restore myself to them when I was wrong. They will remember that I knelt down to them, not who was right.

Restoring Words

The goal of our exchanges is restoration, not being right or wrong. You are making sure the relationship drives the process toward restoration and not forcing restoration to dictate the relationship.

A few sentences you might use with your loved one are:

- "I was wrong to _____"

- "What do you think we need to do to get restored?"

- "I'm willing to offer _____ to make things better."

Restoration is a work of the Spirit, who is our counselor and comforter, so you will want to stay plugged in to ensure you are not doing this in your own thinking or spirit. The mother-daughter relationship is one of the most tender relationships on the planet, so we desperately need the Spirit's leading.

Even if your relationship with your mother or daughter isn't where you want it to be or where it could be based on either one of your desires or expectations, you have the steps to keep pursuing it. You know God says it is important to live restored, as much as it is up to you. Romans 12:18, "If it is possible, as far as it depends on you, live at peace with everyone" (NIV).

How does it depend on you as expressed in this verse? By applying wisdom and understanding in what we know is right. And, ultimately, we depend on God rather than just our own efforts. We reach for the hand that can give us help, without doubting, knowing God brings the ability for us to have purposeful redemption. Proverbs 4:5-6 reminds us: "Get wisdom, get understanding; do not forget my words or swerve from them. Do not forsake wisdom, and she will protect you." How we live at peace depends on gaining wisdom from God and understanding how He brings redemption to us. However, we can also be a barrier to this happening.

Unmended Fences in Restoration

We have heard the expression "mended fences." This implies one or more individuals have improved or repaired a relationship that has been damaged. Do you realize you can actually close yourself off to believing that you can restore your heart to your mother or daughter? In his book *Don't Limit God*, Andrew Wommack talks about how we limit God with our small thinking. He had a radical shift in his life and ministry when he began taking the limits off God. He says, "None of us are believing God and doing everything that we are supposed to be doing. God is big, limitless and infinite; He wants us to believe for big things. Yet most of us only believe for small things."[1]

Are you believing God only for small things in being reunited or joined again in relationship with your mother or daughter? Or are you reaching for big things to happen in your relationship? As you choose the bigger things, remember that not just your actions but your words matter. "Words kill, words give life; they're either poison or fruit—you choose" (Proverbs 18:21 MSG).

If your family mends and my family mends, and then another one mends, our community is going to get stronger. Families are the center. That's why the enemy is so opposed to families. They're so critical.

Restored Heart Even When the Relationship Isn't

Sometimes we don't get the mending we want when we'd like it. But you want to get to a place where you can say, "My heart is mended even if my relationship isn't yet, and I am okay regardless. My peace is not dependent on the other person. My happiness is not up to whether I have a good relationship with my mom or my daughter or not. I'm saying, 'I've done what I can do,' and I'm standing firm with my shoulders back and weight lifted off my shoulders. I know what I believe and I know what I've done, and I stand content in the Lord in my relationship with her." Can you imagine how light our shoulders will feel at this point?

Helen

Even though we learn to look to God for our love, joy, and peace instead of to people, there is grief when things don't turn out like we'd wished for, hoped for. It's a loss. I have spoken with many women who felt as if they were experiencing depression when restoration with their mother or daughter wasn't happening. But I'd ask you to consider this as grief. Grief is the result of loss and change. Making a list of the losses and changes will validate your sadness. But we don't stop there! We take that list before God and ask for more insights, healing, and restoration. The grief list just helps bring more clarity to our hearts as to why we hurt so much. You can have your heart restored, but if there's a tiny corner that's still grieving, it needs to be healed and confessed to God so your restoration is a complete process.

Unexpected Gifts

Darlene Rose was a POW in a Japanese prison camp in New Guinea in the 1940s and is known for saying that her losses were a gift—though not in the wrapping that she would have recognized as a gift. They ended up as a gift for those after her who saw God's faithfulness and redemptive qualities in her life. We aren't saying we are to relish bad things happening to us, but when they happen, God can change our view of the gift wrapping.

Rose shared what she learned from her husband,

> Everything had happened so fast and without the slightest warning! Russell had said, "He will never leave us nor forsake us." No? What about now, Lord? This was one of the times when I thought God had left me, that He had forsaken me. I was to discover, however, that when I took my eyes off the circumstances that were overwhelming me, over which I had no control, and looked up, my Lord was there, standing on the parapet of heaven, looking down. Deep in my heart He whispered, "I'm here. Even

when you don't see Me, I'm here. Never for a moment are you out of My sight."[2]

When Darlene Rose wrote her book, *Evidence Not Seen*, she wrote it with her young sons in mind. "I wished them to know, if ever difficult circumstances came into their lives, that their mother's God is still alive and very well, and His arm has never lost its ancient power."[3]

Friends who have followed Darlene's life and ministry have included this quote on a website attached to her name: "At the beginning of the War, the Lord had given Darlene this verse: Deuteronomy 33:12, 'The beloved of the Lord shall dwell in safety by Him; and the Lord shall cover (overshadow) him all the day long and he shall dwell between His shoulders.' This promise of God was not only the cornerstone of her faith during her internment, but demonstrated that God is able to do abundantly exceedingly above all that she could ask or think as this promise remained the firm foundation of her faith all her days on this earth."[4]

Helen

God has done all that Blythe or I could ask or think in our own relationship. In a way similar to how Rose experienced blessings from her difficulties, the difficulties Blythe and I had over the years ended up as gifts, not in wrappings that we would see as gifts at the time, but they were indeed great gifts to us personally and to future generations of our family. Because of the Lord in our lives, we repaired, mended, and restored areas in our relationship and are able to see the Lord's covering over us as we move forward and bring my grandchildren—Blythe's children and my son Bryan's girls—into the next season of life with us. Sometimes the greatest things we experience come from a place that has caused us pain. And we believe the same is true for you.

My dear daughter-in-law, Lynn, shared,

When hurtful circumstances in life occur that disappoint us deeply, there is a risk for us to withdraw our heart, or even a portion of our heart, from our loved one. Through the power of forgiveness, with the help of Jesus, we can be free. Forgiving our mothers or daughters for their mistakes, shortcomings, and sins while asking the Lord to forgive us for rejecting our mother or daughter helps in the restoration process. Taking on an orphaned identity can be a mind-set that requires taking every thought captive unto the obedience of Christ and renewing our mind. Ask God to take out of you the heart of an orphan and give to you the heart of a daughter (from Ezekiel 36:26) and also Romans 12:2 is central to this: "Do not be conformed to the pattern of this world, but be transformed by the renewing of your mind. Then you will be able to test and approve what God's will is—his good, pleasing and perfect will" (NIV).

Another area that Lynn points out is that

forming judgments contributes to a broken heart. Where we judge another, that judgment can come upon us. For example, a daughter judges her mom for _____, only to find years later she has stepped into the very same action by virtue of the judgment she had against her mom. You'll want to recall what Luke 6:37 says: "Do not judge, and you will not be judged...Forgive, and you will be forgiven" (NIV). In prayer you can place your expectations on the altar of Christ, trusting your good Father to be the source of provision for your soul to rest.

I love this because it's so good and true and God has used Lynn in the lives of many to help them walk this out.

Our good friend Jenny has a story of recovering from a difficult incident as a mother, but she has walked away from any judgments from it. She shares,

> We had recently moved to Chattanooga, Tennessee, for my husband's first job as a youth pastor and camp director at a large church. We had lived in a mobile home in married student housing during seminary and moved with pennies in our pockets but no debt. We were serving a wealthy church. I had a four-year-old son and 18-month-old twin daughters. On Sunday mornings, my husband would go to church early, leaving me the task of feeding and dressing three little ones and making it to church with a smile.
>
> This particular morning my almost-two-year-olds came down the stairs fussing about what shoes to wear. We had two pairs of fancy church shoes, one white pair and one red pair. They were arguing about whose turn it was to wear the red fancy shoes.
>
> I couldn't do it all—breakfast, clothes—with "don't be late" ringing in my ears. I told the girls to go upstairs and figure it out. They came down just minutes later saying, "Each wear one, Mom, each wear one!" It was brilliant. My amazing children had solved their own problem. And I couldn't handle it. I was too insecure, too proud, too worried about what the "church ladies" would think. (And to be honest, it was the 80s and none of us were as free as we are today!) But the problem was me. The mom. I had given the challenge, and my girls accepted! They rose to the occasion, and I squashed them. I totally missed an opportunity to cheer them on in their creativity, their confidence, and their independence.
>
> This story reminds me that although I make mistakes and sometimes choose pride or outward appearance over creative problem-solving and building up my children, Jesus still covers it all. My judgments are covered by His

proclamation that He is bigger—bigger than the missed opportunity of two darling blonde twins wearing one red shoe and one white shoe to church. He is bigger than allowing any part of me to stay there and sorrow in my selfish decision. He is able, and He developed those two little creative minds into the amazing capable adults they are today in spite of their mother!

Jenny said her reaction that morning to make them take off the shoes they put on gave her children the message that it wasn't okay to work things out themselves. But it became a teachable moment. The healing for her as a mom, she said, has been in "admitting to my stubbornness and not listening well to my two-year-olds. That confession then led to further encouragement of their creativity and problem-solving in the days ahead."

Why do we care more about how we are perceived by others rather than how our daughters perceive us? Why do we criticize how our daughter or our mother works it out? If we trust them, we need to let them work it out. Learn to put your trust in your mother when it's appropriate. Extend mercy and love. Let your daughter see how you trust her. Hopefully you can build bridges with her rather than try to rescue her from the other side. Let her come to you. If she doesn't, don't force a path. Let the Holy Spirit bring restoration and nudge both of you in the right timing.

Just Right Recovery

Helen

We have the privilege to pursue recovery. In Scripture when a fish net was repaired, restored, or patched, the word used for this action was *perfect*. No, we're not perfect, but we are patched up with repairs that have made us even stronger. Blythe and I can even finish each other's sentences! Now that's tight!

We can pray for our own wounds and for God to mother us in the places of our hearts where we are missing what we need. How does God do this? How do you expect Him to make up for the places where you are hurting or are not fully healed? What do you want in your relationship with your mom or daughter? Are you leaning on yourself or God to make this happen?

We like how Stasi Eldredge talks about how we can recover from what we didn't get from our mothers. She says,

> Mothers bestow our self-worth, and they have the ability to withhold it…A mother cannot pass on what she does not possess. And neither can we. Mothers have the ability to withhold acceptance, value, love. Our mothers failed us when, without meaning to, they passed on to us low self-esteem. Or based our self-worth on anything other than the fact that we exist.
>
> God does not do that.
>
> Our worth is not based on what we do, which life path we choose, or what we believe. Our worth is inherent in the fact that we are image bearers of the living God.[5]

Mending Thread

Two of the most well-known image bearers of God as mother-in-law and daughter-in-law in the Bible are Ruth and Naomi. They both suffered great losses and were left to figure things out on their own in their new relationship. But as they sought the Lord for their future, God provided for their needs. Their story is a picture of redemption.

One lost a husband; one lost a husband and two sons. Food was scarce where they lived in Moab. Naomi, the mother-in-law, who didn't want to be a burden, we imagine, released her daughters-in-law to go find new husbands and planned to head back to Bethlehem to live and find food there. But Ruth didn't want to leave Naomi and told her that she would stay with her and that Naomi's God would be her God. After they returned, God orchestrated it for Ruth to work in the fields that belonged to Boaz, a relative of Ruth's late father-in-law. He heard she was gleaning the leftover grain, and he let her work safely in his fields and provided water to her.

It was clear to him that Ruth's efforts were to provide and care for Naomi. Their story of restoration and hope spoke volumes. Boaz then acquired the land that was owned by Naomi's late husband, and with it came Naomi and Ruth, and he was able to marry Ruth. They had a son, Jesse, who would be the father of David and from whose genealogy would come Jesus Christ. Boaz is known as "the kinsman redeemer."

God is a restorer. It's clear that even though she didn't have to, Ruth provided for Naomi. And God provided not only for Ruth but for both of them. Probably far above what they both imagined. Their losses were not the end of the story. And look at the impact of their choices and how God's interventions were that He would use Ruth as someone to help bring in the line of David, which would usher in the coming King who would redeem all of us. Now that's a circle, isn't it?

Making It Personal: Recalling God's Promises

Let's look again at God's heart on restoration in these two verses from the beginning of the book:

> Those from among you will rebuild the ancient ruins;
> You will raise up the age-old foundations;
> And you will be called the repairer of the breach,
> The restorer of the streets in which to dwell (Isaiah 58:12).

> Then they will rebuild the ancient ruins,
> They will raise up the former devastations;
> And they will repair the ruined cities,
> The desolations of many generations (Isaiah 61:4).

A restored heart toward God and our family enables us to rebuild and repair our lives. Where do you see God speaking to you about the needs of your heart to restore with Him and with your mother or daughter? What is your first step in this? One way to say this to your mother or daughter is: **"What do you need to see or hear from me for us to have the relationship we both want?"** How will you stay fixed on rebuilding and repairing the breach in your family? What is the motivating factor for you? Stay with this as this will determine your strides as you move forward. Don't lose your footing or your focus, and know there has not been a better time than now or a better initiator than you for your family!

Doing Hard Things Together

Blythe

Constantly doing leaps and practicing cartwheels on a straight line, my younger daughter, Calyn, started increasing her gusto for gymnastics as her first-grade school year came to a close. She had been in class for a while but had taken a year off, and in the year that she started back, she was soaring! She wanted to advance, but no one was really giving us the direction we needed for her to do so. So I hired one of the coaches in the gym, who knew the skill sets needed to advance to the level my older daughter was in, so that she could tell us what Calyn needed in order to go to the next level.

Have you ever hoped for something for your daughter maybe even more than she has? You believe you know what's coming for her and are sure the coach/teacher/instructor will agree?

I watched Calyn do the best she had ever done as the coach led her through warm-ups and skills—some she had never done before—and the coach seemed really impressed. Calyn's practice looked like it was paying off and she was in her element! Her big sister got excited from the balcony as we watched, and our eyes were on Calyn as she leapt into what she loved doing most.

Isn't it amazing to see someone so talented glide through their gifts with seemingly no effort involved? Do you ever sense God has given you something—not just when you were young but now—that you can effortlessly do?

During the moments I watched Calyn, I thought, *This doesn't seem hard for her.* I think that's the way most of us think all of life should be—not difficult when we are doing what God made us to do. We should be able to soar with everything we do because we love God and our children, and yet there's the inconvenient reality that some things are harder than we expected. We have trouble accepting that life is just hard sometimes.

I wasn't expecting the response I got from the coach, and it was hard to hear. Calyn was told that because her strength wasn't quite enough and because of her age, she wouldn't be able to move to the level where her sister had been that would put her on the accelerated track of gymnastics that her sister was on. She was told she would be phenomenal in a different, less competitive program.

The words sat there in our minds for a few minutes while we said our thank-yous and goodbyes and gathered our things and left. Calyn asked me when we got out of the building, "Mama, she said I can't do the program. Why can't I?" I wanted to assure her of her talent but also be truthful with her. It was a moment of doing something hard with her. I was navigating a new area of helping her go her own direction, separate from her sister.

As I gently led her to Starbucks for a calming cappuccino (wait, that was mine!) and a blueberry scone, I quickly let her know what an amazing job she had done. She had shown the coach what she loved doing and how well she could do it. We talked about what the other program would mean for her, and her main question was, "Mama, do I get a team leotard?" She wanted to do floor routines, beam routines, and all of the things she had watched on YouTube videos of other gymnasts. She mainly wanted to know when she could get to it, not how.

In the 30 minutes we had before her regularly scheduled class would start, we talked of dreams and goals and how we could get her on this new path. I cued her up for her current class and talked with the coach she'd been with for a few months who said she would look at Calyn for this other program, which she also coached. As I watched Calyn and gave her a reassuring thumbs-up from the balcony, my own heart began to do flips toward what I could sense God was saying to me. *Do this hard thing with her. Allow Me to show you what good can come from it. Trust Me.*

I began to think about how it could be good for Calyn to be on a different path from her sister so that comparison wouldn't set in. I thought about how much Calyn loves the sport. But what mattered most was how we approached her talent in light of what had been filling up her heart each and every day. There was more here than just gymnastics—there was something in this for us to experience together.

It seemed as though God was moving in this direction for Calyn. Why would I rebuff it? As her mom, could I be trusted to lead her well and to take what was shared with us and process it well with Calyn? This was hard to navigate because it wasn't just a sport or trying not to compare two daughters, it was a life lesson on persevering.

This was a memorable fork in the road where as a mom, I needed to let my daughters be independent of each other and not have them on the same path. Their paths in life would be different in many ways. Letting them be different wasn't hard for them—it just seemed hard for me in trying to keep things on an even level.

You see, I think the blessing of having two daughters is that you have a second chance with the younger what you didn't get right with the first. No, not really, but it seems like a good idea. From birth they have had different personalities, but they love many of the same things and have engaged well with each other with just two years age difference. They each would have hard things come up, and I was supposed to help navigate those things with them.

What I started seeing, even after I talked with Calyn's coach about her moving into this other program when she was ready, is that it's not *how* you get there but *that* you get there. Calyn's eyes are on the goal of her love of going upside down, dancing, and making up routines in her head. She's not concerned with how she gets to do that. She just wants to do it!

Oh, what I learned from an almost-eight-year-old: Focus on the goal, not the measurement stick. For too long I had focused on the measurement with girls in my grade school and high school. Never quite measuring up to what I felt was right and cool and best. I wanted to soar too, and my path often took a much different one from theirs.

As a mom, I don't want my daughters to go through feelings of rejection or not being good enough. None of us do. But we can walk through emotions with them, and we can remind them we are there to do hard things with them. When you go through seasons with your mom or daughter, you can grow together. What comes of harder seasons together is a richness you wouldn't have imagined, growing closer together, learning from each other.

Sometimes walking through hard things together isn't even about how you get out of it but how you relate to each other in it. When you may not even expect it, you can grow stronger together through the difficulties you would not have chosen but are where you find yourself living.

Abiding in the Shadow

Helen

The shadow that fell for me was in the spring of 2017 when I was diagnosed with non-Hodgkin's lymphoma. The tests were shadowy; the long months of chemotherapy very shadowy. The symptoms and setbacks post-chemo and the hospitalizations left me on thin ice. The valley of the shadow was there, but so was my God as I abided in Him. In fact, were it not for Him, I wouldn't have been able to stand. My favorite verse became:

He who dwells in the shelter of the Most High
Will abide in the shadow of the Almighty (Psalm 91:1).

The shadow of the disease was no match for Him who overshadowed me. I learned, too, that the Hebrew for Almighty is "the God of angel armies" and "the God of the armies who fights for his people."[1]

We began to walk by faith, not by sight. This became how I saw each day. I knew God saw me and was with me and that He was asking me to trust Him. I would tell Him I trusted Him for my healing. It was a hard thing that Blythe walked through with me, and it was another level to our relationship we hadn't expected.

Blythe

My brother, Bryan, helped us put our view of our mom in the right perspective as we chose to see the life she possessed. We have a choice in how we see what's in front of us, but sometimes we can speak negatively or hear others speak words that don't bring life to us.

What Bryan shared mirrored how we wanted to live above a diagnosis, how to live embracing something bigger than the moment you are in. His words declared truth about our mother and the hard place we were walking in with her. He shared,

> Father God calls her His child and sees her healed, and that truth, though it's been affirmed by doctors, takes precedence over any circumstance she's having to walk through. Having that faith, to see her as God sees her is a daily need, and she has done it well. A passage that illustrates this well is Romans 4:16-21. Abraham recognized God as the life-giver, as "He who calls that which is not as though it were," literally, calls the things which do not exist as though they do. Paul is not telling Abraham's story so that we deny what is, saying that what we see is not real. Our call is the opposite, to call that which is not yet seen as though it were. That's why he says Abraham faced the facts about his body—he knew what was.

But he becomes the father of faith to all (Romans 4:16) because he did not base his belief in the fulfillment of God's promises on the facts he saw about himself. He grew stronger in faith and gave glory to God. For Mom, the strengthening of her body follows her faith and her confessions of His provision, which is based not in facts and needs, but in what God has done and is doing to restore her.

Jesus doesn't heal partially—He heals fully. When you see people physically and emotionally healed and even see a spiritual transformation, it's always to the core. So it is with our mother and daughter relationship. Jesus heals all the way down to the lowest part of the hard thing in your relationship. Maybe it's not walking through a physically hard time together. It could be things that have been uprooted in your family tree such as verbal exchanges or a long distance in your relationship. And the hard thing for you is deciding when and how to bring it up. Isn't it just easier to do this on our own without involving the other?

Ah, friend. That is the beautiful thing about doing hard things. You don't have to do them alone. You are meant to do them with those you love, and we want to see you be able to do this with your mother or daughter.

Love in Sharper Focus

Blythe

The hard things Mom and I went through in our years together brought our love in sharper focus. Mom had always cheered me on, showed me truths, and been a confident leader of her heart and mine. Sometimes it felt like she had faith when I didn't. In the season of walking with her through lymphoma, I found myself in a hard place of being the one encouraging her and speaking life over her and encouraging her to press forward and make the words of our vertical relationship to God more than our horizontal noticings of the physical place she was in.

Doing hard things brought us nearer to each other's heart. When you see you are in a position to help the other, it changes things. When you see that life would not be the same without her, it changes your perspective. I didn't think I might physically lose her, but I thought life might not look the same with how Mom lives life. And that crumbled my heart because of the life I wanted to continue with her.

I think when we realize what was and what might not be, we quicken our resolve to live without holding back. And I wanted to make the best of walking a hard road together by being aware of Mom's challenges, but also not letting them define her or her situation.

Sometimes daughters have to be the mothers speaking truth over the other and holding on to hope for both of you. Some seasons require this. And that can feel backward and difficult to experience when you've always been the daughter. But there is a spiritual principle at work.

When Jesus called His disciples, He asked them if they loved Him. The disciples left families, work, callings, and a place of comfort to confront the good, hard things with Jesus. They walked long days together, went into sticky situations with Jesus, had to figure out how to distribute food, had to help decide who needed to be healed and who could get close to Jesus. It wasn't a life of gratitude. But it was a life of privilege.

And we have that same life of privilege to experience with our mother or daughter. God assigned them to us. He must have known we could do this together.

What if your mother or daughter won't allow you to travel a hard road with her? What do you do? You can offer. And offer again. And pray for the softening of her heart so she'll be open to you and allow you to do hard things together. You can't push the door down to do so.

And you don't want to close the door on doing hard things together because you don't think she'd even consider coming to your side. Pressing in and being available signals you are moving toward her. You will not be able to stay in the same place you are in and do hard things together. It forces you to move. And it will draw you closer or pull you apart. We want to inspire you to move closer to her even if it's not reciprocated.

You may not be walking through cancer together. You might be talking with your mom about losing her spouse. You could be walking a hard path of putting your mother in a nursing facility. Your daughter might need you to help raise her child because she can't do it as a single mom. Your daughter may have news to tell you she doesn't think you can hear and handle. The hard road you are walking may be telling each other how you feel about the other and that you are uncertain about the road you are walking in the future together.

But here's truth: You can do this! As God's child, He has empowered you to do hard things together with your mother or daughter. You are not alone. And we don't want you to think that hard means bad. Hard can also be viewed as "good coming." Because we know we will not stay in hard forever. Jesus rose from the dead. There is life from death. But we have to seek it. There can be good in the hard, but are we looking for it?

A dear friend and trusted soul talked with me before I was going to go be with my mom on a visit where she was going to be in a more weakened state than the last time I had seen her. Mom was working diligently to return to the state of life she was in before her chemo journey began. And this was a difficult road to walk, mainly for her to push ahead toward life, and for me as a daughter in another state, 1,200 miles away.

Others have said that chemo robs you of everything in order to allow you to build back up. And while that may be true, I didn't want to focus on the tearing-down part but the building back up. That is, after all, what we had been talking about when we were writing our book as her chemo journey began.

I appreciated the truth my thoughtful friend offered one night. "It will be hard but holy." And through tears, I acknowledged this to be true. I have shed a lot of tears in this season, unbeknownst to Mom. Initially my tears would come not when I was on the phone with her or in her presence but after. It wasn't that I was trying to hide anything, but I did feel a strong surge of peace when I was around her or talking with her. It was as if I could be a stronger voice for her than the words she could express herself.

But then in the presence of friends or in front of my husband and children, I was the one who felt the weight and the change in our relationship in the day to day and it felt crushing. Later two dear people who prayed for me said they felt as though I had a burden on my back that I needed to let go. And when I realized others could see this, I did pray to let it go.

During some of this time I didn't have the gift of freely texting, emailing, or calling Mom whenever I wanted to. Calls were less. Texts were through my dad. Our communication was affected, and our ability to connect on a deeper level was affected. But we had life! And we still had the gift of our time together. Mom was starting over in many ways. Reintroducing foods. Learning to walk again. And in the words we got to exchange before she would need to rest from exhaustion, I would try to speak truth and bring words she could affirm by her own confessions. Sometimes it was a prayer. Sometimes it was simply, "I love you, Mom, and you can do this. Jesus has provided all you need. He has paid for your healing."

There was hard, yes. But there was also holy. Jesus was right in the midst of our lives. He was there to receive our weary hearts as we pressed into Him for our breath and being each day. And it is holy ground to walk on when you see Jesus sustaining and restoring. There wasn't any other explanation. And there wasn't any other way to live.

Choosing to See God in the Hard

Blythe

I remember how well Mom had done this with me, going through a hard season together. Mom had been with me through my hard. In the fall of 2006, we lost our first baby through miscarriage and my husband's birth mother all in the same week. Mom came out to be with us while my husband's birth mother was in hospice, and Mom walked with me through the doctor visit and subsequent time of saying goodbye to our baby and Art's birth mother. At the time I was working with Ransomed Heart Ministries, which was founded by John and Stasi Eldredge, and this great company of men and women gave us a lot of support. One of the key phrases I remember John Eldredge sharing with me during that time was this: "Sometimes in life you can either have God or understanding. But very rarely do you get both." I chose God, even when my heart didn't understand. *Why did I have to lose our baby? Couldn't God have prevented this?* Why did losing someone you had never met hurt so much? If we were to have another baby, how would I get through the hard part of remembering?

I remember going to the first ultrasound with our second baby and now older daughter, Maris, and I held my hands open, saying, "Lord, You have me and You have this baby." I loved my daughter before she was born because I knew the cost of losing my first daughter. And I wanted so very much to do this hard thing of holding trust and peace in my hands rather than fear.

A few years after Maris was born, we gained another daughter—and a son. When our twins were six weeks old, I started hemorrhaging in our pediatrician's office while my husband was taking my parents to the airport after they had been with us helping for six weeks. They flew home, and then Mom turned around and came back out to help during the hospitalizations and surgeries I had. She took care of my babies and took care of me. She walked me through some really hard days, always with hope and reassurance for the life God had given me and the goodness of His provisions.

As she and I have said, we have both been in desperate situations, and we were desperate for God. There was something about our going to new levels in our place with God and with each other. How do you partner together in the hard? You focus on what's common between you: life.

When you focus on what's most important, suddenly the things you wish you would have said or what you want to experience takes a front seat. Anything you might have built up between you isn't so important. The importance is life and how you seek it.

One of the key ways we recommend doing this is to take a step back. One of the best gifts you can give your relationship and each other in the hard place is rest.

Rest

There is a pause that refreshes and restores. And if you look closely at the word *restore*, which we have been focusing on in this book, rest is right there in it.

You cannot survive the relationship if you are striving as mother and daughter. Instead of always working hard in your relationship and in the place you may find yourself now, you will want to simply rest in your life and in your relationship as mother and daughter. What does rest look like? We think you can do several things that can bring your relationship into a place where you both feel lighter and not weighed down by the things between you:

1. Lighten the load between you by letting go of lesser important things.

2. Find the occasions to just talk about your relationship.

3. Create something between you to feel good about: a project or an occasion to celebrate a child/grandchild.

4. Resist the urge to talk negatively of the other.

5. Let down defenses and pick up unconditional acceptance.

6. Remember that what you think and speak can negatively impact the outcome.

John 15 looks at resting in Jesus, and John says twice in this passage, "Love one another." The secret to loving is abiding in Him. Jesus commanded us to love one another. It's not just a good idea but a command. When you abide in Him, you are saying, "You have my affection and attention more than my situation." And when you put Him above the magnitude of the hard, you will not be unthreaded. The hard may get harder, but you are mended to God. Your heart toward your mother or daughter should not be pulled apart but made tighter.

See, there are two sides in a drawing of a heart. Think about the hearts you cut out of construction paper as a child. When you draw a line down the middle, the two sides reflect each other, and when joined, they make a whole. Whole means there is no lack. Even when you are doing hard things together, despite the outcome of your hard, you have a completed, restored, and whole heart. And no matter who draws around your heart, your life and your heart don't change in shape but in capacity.

The process of mending your heart with your mother's or daughter's is the result of the time you have pressed into loving her not for who she is but who she is becoming. When what's been between you moves from a difficult hard to a beautiful hard, and when you experience the beautiful hard of turning your heart to love in a way you haven't before and for the first time seeing how you can be loved in return—now this is restoration. This is the kind of heart rebuilding that is the greatest level of sacrifice, risk, and reward we want every mother and daughter to have. When you expect and affirm your belief, you can see the repair you want in your relationship. God goes to the most extravagant lengths to move and shift things from your asking to building these realities, such as a renewed love for your mom or daughter, into your life. He's a God who never tires of waiting or fulfilling. Are you ready to initiate this kind of restoration He is offering you?

Mending Thread

How does doing something hard together bring you closer? Are you stuck in the hard, or are you moving through it with hope?

Look ahead to the vision of what you want to see. If you don't look for it and call it, you won't be able to take steps to reach it. Call it by name so you know where you are wanting to travel in your relationship. It may help to write it out as a vision statement of your life with your mother or daughter.

You do all you can and then you take the biblical command to stand. Ephesians 6:13 talks about "having done everything, to stand firm." You will never know how you can initiate repair with your mother or daughter if you don't try. Your relationship now is not the end of your story. You don't know what's coming down the road. Starting the journey is pivotal. Ask God to help you as you seek to bring the hard you have encountered into a closer union with each other.

Making It Personal: Making an Invitation

Make an invitation and send it to your mother or daughter. You might want to use words like, "I invite you to let me join you in doing this hard thing with you."

It is a declaration of intent to love and push through the hard things together. Or write a letter from your mother or daughter to yourself where you have invited yourself into her life to do hard things with her. If she is not open at the time, you have purposed in your heart and you have stepped out in faith. Continue to pray for open doors to talk with her. Be the healthy one in the relationship and watch humility at work. If you aren't able to share the invitation with your mother or daughter, maybe share it with a sister or a child and invite them to do something hard with you. In this, you are repairing and restoring a new generation.

Proactively Pray for the Protection of Your Relationship

We want to encourage you to consider one more thing in your journey of mending your heart with your mother or daughter. Would you consider praying a prayer for protection of your relationship? Whatever level it's on or stage it's in, it still needs supernatural protection. We want to leave a prayer for you here, but you can adapt it and make it your own:

Father God, I place myself under the divine authority that You hold, both eternally and in my life. I bring the relationship with my mother/daughter under the reign and rule of Your kingdom and declare that it is redeemed and restored and according to Isaiah 58:12. You have rebuilt the ancient ruins, You have raised up the former foundations, and You have repaired the breach between me and my family. You are the restorer in whom I dwell. You dwell in me, and I am in You. I place a supernatural covering over my relationship with my mother/daughter, and while I refute the former things between us, I usher in the new things You have done and will continue to do in my relationship with her. Keep my words pure, help me reach the level of oneness that I know exists for us, and keep my mind fixed on You and no one or nothing else. In You I find my life. You will complete what You have started, and in the name, power, and authority of Jesus Christ I take my place as Your child before You and surrender my relationship with my mother/daughter to You for Your active work in my heart to honor her and You in my life. Amen.

Afterword

Blythe

In the journey of writing this book, Mom and I stretched our relationship more than we thought we would. We started writing as Mom was diagnosed with lymphoma, which we didn't know at the time would bring us closer than we could have expected. Mom would write on days when she felt well enough to get to her computer during chemo treatments. But what happened next was nothing short of a miracle. During Mom's stay in a rehabilitation hospital after the symptoms from chemo caused a debilitating low, I would sit and listen to her and type the words she would speak. Having Parkinson's as well, her handwriting had been shaky, but it was starting to come back. She wrote out things for me to include, and it was like gold in my hands.

Friend, we didn't know that in writing a book together, it would take us deeper into places we needed to address. Or in moments of seeking life when others told us Mom may not return to the place she was before that we would be saying and doing things we couldn't have pictured in a season when we had experienced vitality of life. During months of sickness and learning how to walk again and eat again without the assistance of feedings, Mom was encouraging me and inspiring me in ways I'll never forget. Our hearts were joined even further in the hard. And the hard things didn't pull us away. For this, we are grateful, for often hard things can drive families apart.

My admonition to you is to trust the hard places, lean in as close as you can, and let God surprise you with how you can come out with a deeper love for your mother or daughter than you ever expected. Just as Mom and I take literal steps together with her holding on to me as she finds her footing again, may you come up alongside your mother or daughter and hold on to her and the hope you have for a relationship you may not imagine right now, but it can come. And oh, the goodness of it even if it doesn't reach the length or depth of the places you'd like it to. We can be grateful for what we do have.

At the time of our concluding the writing of this book, I was spending the last days with my mother-in-law. As I was telling her how much I loved her and her son and how grateful I was to be in their family, through labored breathing, she said, "Thank you for your love."

I started thinking about how we look at our relationship with a mother, mother-in-law, daughter, daughter-in-law and how we live in one moment with any of these is a decision away from reaping a benefit or a loss—the benefit of a relationship that is breathing life or the loss of a moment together because we can't bring ourselves to do it.

Life is not measured in the big or even final moments but in the little moments and decisions leading up to the bigger moments. Sometimes we speak into each other's lives through all of those smaller decisions and words and ordinary times we have invested in. And they add up to an impact the person will carry with them the rest of their life, even if they can only share a few words recognizing it.

So use every opportunity you have to draw closer, because you don't know the influence that any and every gesture can have. It's a life you won't regret. We pray you make great strides in your relationship with your mother or daughter and walk in places you never knew could be yours!

Appendix A

Healing the Brokenness
(used with permission from www.ransomedheart.com)

Healing doesn't necessarily have to be dramatic. Oftentimes it is very quiet. Jesus simply comes as we invite him to, and though we may not "see" him or "hear" him, he comes, and we sense a new peace or quietness in our soul. Our heart feels better somehow. The important thing is for us to give him permission to these wounded places, invite his healing love, and wait in prayer for him to come. Do this with each memory of wounding, with each event (ask the Holy Spirit to guide you). Often I will pray Isaiah 61 as I do this:

Lord Jesus, you have come to heal the brokenhearted, to proclaim freedom for the captives and release from darkness for the prisoners, to proclaim the year of the Lord's favor and the day of vengeance of our God. Come and heal my brokenness right here, Lord; free me from this captivity, release me from all darkness, bring your favor here in my soul and bring your vengeance here against my enemies. Lord, you came to comfort all who mourn, and provide for those who grieve in Zion—to bestow on them a crown of beauty instead of ashes, the oil of gladness instead of mourning, and a garment of praise instead of a spirit of despair. I ask you to do this in me— comfort me where I am hurting; bestow on me a crown of beauty instead of ashes, the oil of gladness instead of mourning, and a garment of praise instead of a spirit of despair. Come in this memory, in this wound. I receive you here.

Many times Jesus simply says, "Let me love you." We need to open our hearts up to his love. As we do, it allows him to come to this very place. Linger there and listen; ask for the healing grace of Jesus Christ over and over again. He comes, dear friends, he comes.

See more at www.ransomedheart.com/prayer

Appendix B

Expanded List of Verses from Chapter 3
on Listening Well to Others

Those who guard their lips preserve their lives, but those who speak rashly will come to ruin (Proverbs 13:3 NIV).

Even fools are thought wise if they keep silent, and discerning if they hold their tongues (Proverbs 17:28 NIV).

The soothing tongue is a tree of life, but a perverse tongue crushes the spirit (Proverbs 15:4 NIV).

Speak up for those who cannot speak for themselves, for the rights of all who are destitute (Proverbs 31:8 NIV).

But I tell you that everyone will have to give account on the day of judgment for every empty word they have spoken (Matthew 12:36 NIV).

Sin is not ended by multiplying words, but the prudent hold their tongues (Proverbs 10:19 NIV).

My mouth is filled with your praise, declaring your splendor all day long (Psalm 71:8 NIV).

May these words of my mouth and this meditation of my heart be pleasing in your sight, LORD, my Rock and my Redeemer (Psalm 19:14 NIV).

The lips of the righteous know what finds favor, but the mouth of the wicked only what is perverse (Proverbs 10:32 NIV).

Whoever conceals hatred with lying lips and spreads slander is a fool (Proverbs 10:18 NIV).

The lips of fools bring them strife, and their mouths invite a beating (Proverbs 18:6 NIV).

A gossip betrays a confidence, but a trustworthy person keeps a secret (Proverbs 11:13 NIV).

Words from the mouth of the wise are gracious, but fools are consumed by their own lips (Ecclesiastes 10:12 NIV).

What you have said in the dark will be heard in the daylight, and what you have whispered in the ear in the inner rooms will be proclaimed from the roofs (Luke 12:3 NIV).

Out of the same mouth come praise and cursing. My brothers and sisters, this should not be (James 3:10 NIV).

Fools find no pleasure in understanding but delight in airing their own opinions (Proverbs 18:2 NIV).

Save me, LORD, from lying lips and from deceitful tongues (Psalm 120:2 NIV).

If I speak in the tongues of men or of angels, but do not have love, I am only a resounding gong or a clanging cymbal (1 Corinthians 13:1 NIV).

Anxiety weighs down the heart, but a kind word cheers it up (Proverbs 12:25 NIV).

The tongue has the power of life and death, and those who love it will eat its fruit (Proverbs 18:21 NIV).

A person finds joy in giving an apt reply—and how good is a timely word! (Proverbs 15:23 NIV).

If your brother or sister sins, go and point out their fault, just between the two of you. If they listen to you, you have won them over (Matthew 18:15 NIV).

We all stumble in many ways. Anyone who is never at fault in what they say is perfect, able to keep their whole body in check (James 3:2 NIV).

How God Wants to Speak to Us

And Eli said to Samuel, "Go lie down, and it shall be if He calls you, that you shall say, 'Speak, LORD, for Your servant is listening.'" So Samuel went and lay down in his place. Then the LORD came and stood and called as at other times, "Samuel! Samuel!" And Samuel said, "Speak, for Your servant is listening" (1 Samuel 3:9-10).

To him the doorkeeper opens, and the sheep hear his voice, and he calls his own sheep by name and leads them out. When he puts forth all his own, he goes ahead of them, and the sheep follow him because they know his voice...I have other sheep, which are not of this fold; I must bring them also, and they will hear My voice; and they will become one flock *with* one shepherd...My sheep hear My voice, and I know them, and they follow Me (John 10:3,4,16,27).

I will instruct you and teach you in the way which you should go; I will counsel you with My eye upon you (Psalm 32:8).

Generational Patterns

You shall not make for yourself an idol, or any likeness of what is in heaven above or on the earth beneath or in the water under the earth. You shall not worship them or serve them; for I, the LORD your God, am a jealous God, visiting the iniquity of the fathers on the children, on the third and the fourth generations of those who hate Me (Exodus 20:4-5).

You shall not worship them or serve them; for I, the LORD your God, am a jealous God, visiting the iniquity of the fathers on the children, and on the third and the fourth generations of those who hate Me (Deuteronomy 5:9).

The LORD is slow to anger and abundant in lovingkindness, forgiving iniquity and transgression; but He will by no means clear the guilty, visiting the iniquity of the fathers on the children to the third and the fourth generations (Numbers 14:18).

For He established a testimony in Jacob and appointed a law in Israel, which He commanded our fathers that they should teach them to their children, that the generation to come might know, even the children yet to be born, that they may arise and tell them to their children, that they should put their confidence in God and not forget the works of God, but keep His commandments, and not be like their fathers, a stubborn and rebellious generation, a generation that did not prepare its heart and whose spirit was not faithful to God (Psalm 78:5-8).

One generation shall commend your works to another, and shall declare your mighty acts (Psalm 145:4 ESV).

Notes

Chapter 1

1. Stasi Eldredge, *Becoming Myself* (Colorado Springs, CO: David C. Cook, 2014), 75-76.

Chapter 2

1. Misty S. Bledsoe, "The Meaning of Stones in the Bible," https://classroom.syn onym.com/the-meaning-of-stones-in-the-bible-12082596.html, September 29, 2017.

Chapter 5

1. https://www.alcoholics-anonymous.org.uk/About-AA/The-12-Steps-of-AA
2. Lewis B. Smedes, *Forgive and Forget* (San Francisco, CA: HarperOne: 1996), 133.
3. Mark Cowart, "Vision: What Do You See?" Sermon, Church for All Nations, Colorado Springs, CO, January 21, 2018.
4. Ibid.

Chapter 6

1. Cindy Jacobs, "Word of the Lord—2018," generals.org, January 15, 2018, CharismaMag.com reprinted from https://www.generals.org/articles/single/word-of-the-lord-2018/

Chapter 7

1. https://en.wikiquote.org/wiki/Willy_Wonka_%26_the_Chocolate_Factory
2. Ibid.

Chapter 9

1. Eldredge, *Becoming Myself*, 47.
2. Ibid., 73.
3. Andrew Wommack, *Don't Limit God* (Tulsa, OK: Harrison House Publishers, 2014), 106-07.
4. Ibid., 107.

Chapter 10

1. Wommack, *Don't Limit God*, 7.
2. Darlene Rose, *Evidence Not Seen: A Woman's Miraculous Faith in the Jungles of World War II* (New York, NY: Harper Collins, 2003), 46.
3. Darlene Rose, darlenerose.org/ministry news.html
4. Dr. and Mrs. William K. Henry, darlenerose.org, January 2007, http://darlenerose.org
5. Eldredge, *Becoming Myself*, 84.

Chapter 11

1. https://www.spencerdailyreporter.com/story/1945830.html and http://names forgod.net/god-of-hosts/

Acknowledgments

We bow our knees before the Father in earnest and deepest thanks for His mending in us and for His words to share. We thank our adored family and friends for their love and support. There are no words adequate enough to express our love and appreciation. We thank our glorious publisher Harvest House and their amazing team for putting our mended pieces together and for the hands who brought this book to life.

We thank our launch team, endorsers, and story contributors with our whole hearts. And you, the reader—we acknowledge you too! We wrote this book for you...

Helen:

Thank you, Blythe, for being the Best Ever Agent in the whole wide world. I love you as my agent and my partner in writing.

Jim, I love you for supporting me and helping me as I wrote and saw this book to completion. Thank you for mailing things and holding me up with your offers of help to me.

Blythe:

Thank you, Mom, for giving me the opportunity to do something I have always wanted to do in writing a book with you to share how God has intervened in our story. You are a treasure!

Art, thank you for letting me pursue my dream of writing a book and for all the nights you fixed the kids dinner and got them to bed so I could work on the book. I love you endlessly!

Stephanie Alton and my BDA clients, thank you for supporting me through the process of writing and for helping Mom and me as we set sail as authors.

John and Stasi Eldredge, thank you for the gift of life you have taught me to seize. And for your heart for me in the years I have learned from you. I am so grateful for you and love you.

Michael and Gail Hyatt, thank you for modeling to me what it means to be a writer and parents who invest in your daughters. I appreciate all the wisdom and love you have given me.

About the Authors

Blythe Daniel is a literary agent and marketer with 20-plus years of experience in publishing. She is a speaker at writer's conferences and is interviewed for podcasts and webinars. She has written for *Christian Retailing* and *Focus on the Family* publications, and she links hundreds of bloggers with millions of readers through BlogAbout. Her passion is helping authors share their unique stories. The daughter of Dr. Helen McIntosh, she lives in Colorado with her husband and three children.

Dr. Helen McIntosh (EdD, Counseling Psychology) is a counselor, speaker, and educator, and has authored books on self-image and conflict resolution: *Messages to Myself* and *Eric, Jose & The Peace Rug®*. Her work has appeared in several national outlets including *Guideposts*, *ParentLife*, and *HomeLife* magazines. She resides in Dalton, Georgia, with her husband, Jim. They have two children, son Bryan and daughter Blythe McIntosh Daniel, and are grandparents five times over.